READING THE TAROT

LEO LOUIS MARTELLO

AVERY PUBLISHING GROUP INC.

Garden City Park, New York

Cover Design: Rudy Shur and Martin Hochberg
Cover Painting: Michael Apici
In-House Editor: Karen Price

Library of Congress Cataloging-in-Publication Data

Martello, Leo Louis.
   Reading the Tarot : understanding the cards of destiny / Leo Louis
Martello.
     p.   cm.
   Includes bibliographical references.
   ISBN 0-89529-441-9
   BF1879.T2M36   1990
   133.3'2424--dc20   89-494121
                                         CIP

Printed in the United States of America

10 9 8 7

CONTENTS

To my Sicilian Grandmother,
Maria Concetta Martello

INTRODUCTION

The Tarot cards used in this book were originally drawn by artist Pamela Colman Smith for A. E. Waite's book *The Pictorial Key to the Tarot*, published in 1910. The reading methods used in this book are not Waite's, with whom I'm often in profound disagreement, as evidenced by some of my comments. Though he was a brilliant student of all of the occult and magickal systems, he had his blind spots. Some of them I point out in this book.

The reading method used is an accumulation of card meanings, symbology, Gypsy divination, occult knowledge, and personal experience. Old meanings have been updated. When I first was taught to read the Tarot by my Gypsy friend Marta over forty years ago, these cards weren't as popular as they are today. Now they are almost an integral part of the New Age movement. All kinds of special interest decks are being published, such as decks dealing with feminism and/or witches, and those illustrated by artist Salvador Dali. *The Book Of Thoth* was a name given to the Tarot cards by Count de Gebelin in the eighteenth century. In 1944, Aleister Crowley self-published a book using this title.

The primary purpose of this book is to show you how to *read* the Tarot, how to make sense out of the cards, and how to use them in a practical way. And, although the Tarot has been used for centuries for deeper esoteric and philosophical insights, whole books could be written on the symbolism of each card in the Major Arcana. The average person wants immediate guidance and solutions to problems. Health, home, and happiness; family, friends, and finances; love, loneliness, and luck; all the things that go into everyday living. The Tarot reader has been called "the poor man's psychiatrist." Most people simply need someone to talk to, a trusted confidant, a helping hand when there is no one else to turn to. The reader doesn't have to be Nostradamus—just sincere, knowledgeable, and a good listener. As Napoleon once said: "The wonderful thing about a prophet is that he can't be disputed!"

I have been reading Tarot cards as well as the regular deck of fifty-two cards for over forty years, and the interpretations given in the Minor Arcana in this book can be used to read the latter. In 1964, I spent a year in Tangier, Morocco, where I tried to trace the origins of the Tarot, notably in the ancient city of Fez, and in other travels throughout North Africa, Italy, and Sicily. I'm indebted to no specific person but rather to all of those Tarot originators, authors, and readers who have gone before me, and to the thousands of clients I've read over the years. In many ways, the Tarot has been my catechism for counselling. May you derive as much satisfaction out of the Tarot as I have.

One

Historical Background

The seventy-eight cards of the Tarot have been used for centuries to reveal the mysteries and patterns of the past and the events of the future.

The history of Tarot cards parallels the history of printing in Europe. In the fourteenth century, Spanish monks were printing with wooden blocks cut with letters. They would press the ink-dipped blocks on manuscript paper. The next step in the history of printing was the use of wooden blocks that printed playing cards and, later, religious pictures, designs, fabrics, and entire words. Then, in 1440, Johann Gutenberg of Mainz, Germany invented movable type. With this invention, cards were mass-produced in Europe. Tarot cards became more popular and new games were introduced.

Tarot cards were called "devil's pasteboards" in the Dark Ages, when the Inquisition made the reading of them a crime punishable by death by burning at the stake. In 1404, the Catholic Church forbade their priests to even touch the cards. Yet it was during this period that card making became a regular trade in Germany. This country even had its own Card Maker's Guild.

THE ORIGIN OF THE CARDS

The origin of the Tarot is shrouded in mystery. There are
many theories as to where the cards originated. One is that
they originated in the Egyptian Mystery schools, which
reduced universal truths into hieroglyphic tablets, de-
cipherable only to initiates. The man who popularized this
theory was a famous hairdresser by the name of Alliette,
who practiced during the French Revolution. His first book
appeared in 1783 under the name of Etteilla (his name
spelled backwards). He wrote:

> On a table or altar in the temple of Ftah in Memphis,
> at the height of the breast of the Egyptian Magus,
> where, on one side, a book or collection of cards, or
> plates of gold (the tarots) and on the other a vase. . . .

He claimed that the word "tarot" is derived from the
pure Egyptian word *Tar*, a path, and *Ro, Ros, Rog*, meaning
royal, and that the two together mean "The Royal Path of
Life."

Another proponent of this theory, Count de Gebelin,
an eighteenth century writer commenting on *The Book of
Thoth* (which is another name for the Tarot), wrote:

> If it were known that there exists in our day a work
> of the ancient Egyptians, which had escaped the
> flames that devoured their superb libraries, and which
> contains their purest doctrines on the most interesting
> subjects, every one would doubtless be anxious to ac-
> quire the secrets of so valuable a work. . . . This work
> is composed of 78 illustrations. . . .

Count de Gebelin claimed that he found remnants of
ancient Egyptian knowledge in the old Italian Tarocchi
(Tarot) cards, but that they had been so changed and dis-
torted that the true meanings and original knowledge had
been lost and the cards had become common playthings.
One group of people to whom this knowledge was *not* lost
were the Italian-Sicilian witches, or *strege* (and only a few

of them at that). My paternal grandmother and great-grandmother were both local *strege*. Besides having knowledge of herbs, healing, the power of suggestion, magickal spells, and good horse-sense psychology, they were readers of the Tarocchi deck of cards. It is also a known fact that the ancient Egyptians and Phoenicians sailed the Mediterranean and often traded with the Maltese and the Sicilians. Even today, Maltese fishermen have the Eye of Horus painted on their boats, though I doubt that they are aware of its origin.

My family is predominantly Sicilian, with some Italians. The former have traces of Arabian, Phoenician, and Egyptian blood, and are proud of their heritage. Their religion, their rites, and their gods were *not* of the Romans. Even during the pre-Christian times, the worship practices of the Sicilians were secret and operated as an underground faith. One writer, Charles Godfrey Leland, author of *Aradia, The Gospel of the Witches* (1892), discovered that the worship of the goddess Diana is still prevalent throughout Italy, and came closer than any other author to the truth, that the *strege* were descendants of Europe's pagan religions. The High Priestess card in the Tarot is representative of their goddess Diana (who is called another name by initiates). Waite has called this "the memorial of some popular superstition," which shows how little he knew. He is correct only if you take the view that all religions are nothing but superstition. His arbitrary statement was not based on personal knowledge, scholarship, or research.

Another scholar who believes that the cards originated in Egypt was Samuel Liddell MacGregor Mathers, one-time head of the Hermetic Order of the Golden Dawn. This secret society, which originated in England, had as its goal the revival of the practices of Alchemy and other practices of the occult, along with the study of the deeper meanings of the Tarot, Astrology, and Numerology. Liddell has written that the word "tarot" is derived from the Egyptian word *taru*, meaning "to require an answer" or "to consult."

He explains that the last *t* is added to indicate that the
gender is feminine.

A second theory on the origin of the Tarot ascribes it
to the Gypsies. One writer, De l'Hoste Ranking, says that
the word "tarot" is derived from the Hungarian Gypsy
word *tar*, meaning a pack of cards, and this in turn was
derived from the Hindustani *taru*. He calls the theories of
Etteilla, de Gebelin, and others "worthless."

The writer Vaillant lived with the Gypsies for many years
and wrote a series of books on the subject from 1853 to
1863. The later writer, Papus who wrote *The Tarot of the
Bohemians*, was much influenced by him, and wrote in 1889:

> The Gypsies possess a Bible, yes, this card game called
> the Tarot which the Gypsies possess is the Bible of
> Bibles. It is a marvelous book, as Count de Gebelin
> and especially Vaillant have realized. Under the names
> of Tarot, Thora, Roa, this game has formed succes-
> sively the basis of the synthetic teaching of all the
> ancient peoples.

Though Ranking rejects their theories, he did write in
1908:

> I would submit, that from internal evidence we may
> deduce that the *tarots* were introduced by a race speak-
> ing an Indian dialect; that the form of the Pope (as
> portrayed in the *tarots*) shows they had been long in
> a country where the orthodox Eastern Church pre-
> dominated; and the form of headdress of the King,
> together with the shape of the eagle on the shield,
> shows that this was governed by Russian Grand Dukes,
> who had not yet assumed the Imperial insignia. This
> seems to me confirmatory of the widespread belief
> that it is to the Gypsies we are indebted for our knowl-
> edge of playing cards.

One writer, Wilshire, in his *Descriptive Catalogues of Cards
in the British Museum*, 1877, refutes the above. He says:

.

"Whether the Zingarie (Gypsies) be of Egyptian or Indian origin, they did not appear in Europe before 1417, when cards had been known for some time." But he's wrong about this, as Gypsies had been in Europe long, long before that date. In fact, they held a Gypsy barony on the island of Corfu in the fourteenth century.

A third theory on the origin of the Tarot is that it descended from the Hebrew Cabala, developed as a pictorial form of the secret teachings to simplify learning for the initiates. The Waite deck, which is used in this book and was drawn by artist Pamela Colman Smith, is full of Cabalistic symbols, especially the Wheel of Fortune with its Hebrew inscriptions and the Hebrew yods shown descending on The Moon and The Tower cards. Waite and Smith were both members of the Hermetic Order of the Golden Dawn. Waite's vows to the Order prevented him from coming right out and saying that these are cabalistic symbols.

A fourth rather esoteric theory is that the Tarot are the remnants of the lost continent of Atlantis, when the priests inscribed all their knowledge on tablets in the hope that they would be salvaged after the continent's destruction.

A fifth theory deals with Jung's idea of the collective unconscious—universal symbolism, that storehouse of knowledge inherent in the unconscious mind of all people.

My own view is that various cultures had designed certain cards independently of one another. The designs are characteristic of each culture, similar to the primitive cave drawings found around the world, and to the art in the pyramids of Egypt and North America. The desire for self-expression is a universal trait. The traditions were handed down orally, some carved on rocks and in caves, others on obelisks, tablets, and totem poles, and eventually on wood, parchment, and paper when this was available. During early times, tradesmen and travelers could have picked up such cards, brought them back to their own countries, recopied them, and, during the course of this, changed the symbolism to coincide with their own cultures.

During the Crusades, many Knights Templars brought back such cards from the East. This constant intercourse between East and West was certainly conducive to the introduction of such "oddities" as painted, gilded, and ornamental cards.

I spent most of 1964 in Morocco, and one of my hopes was to be able to trace the origin of the Tarot at the University of Fez, where I had many friends. However, I had little time and so much to do. Also, I spoke mostly in French and broken Arabic and was unable to read the ancient Arabic manuscripts, so this proved fruitless. I was struck by the fact that their ordinary playing cards resembled a modified Tarot, and learned to play with my Moroccan friends. I was ever conscious of the fact that the Arabs and Moors introduced these cards into Spain when they conquered that country.

Waite has written, "If the Tarot were of fortune telling in the root-matter thereof, we should have to look in very strange places for the motive which devised it—to Witchcraft and the Black Sabbath, rather than any Secret Doctrine." Waite may have been fully versed in the rituals of the Order of the Golden Dawn, but he does not seem to realize that witchcraft and the Black Sabbath are *not* one and the same, and that calling these "strange places" reveals his ignorance about the Old Religion.

Still, Waite makes a valid point, even if his knowledge of the old Religion is spotty. This point is that the Tarot is much more than just a method of fortune telling by cards. I fully agree with this. Waite also writes:

> There is a Secret Tradition concerning the Tarot, as well as a Secret Doctrine contained therein; I have followed some part of it without exceeding the limits which are drawn about matters of this kind and belong to the laws of honour. This tradition has two parts, and as one of them has passed into writing it seems to follow that it may be betrayed at any moment, which

will not signify, because the second, as I have intimated, has not so passed at present and is held by very few indeed.

There is absolutely no proof that the Tarot was originated by witches, but it is true that in the Craft there have always been Secret Doctrines and Traditions that have never been put on paper and about which Waite knew nothing. These Secret Doctrines and Traditions are continued today by most Traditionalist and Continental witches. This is not true of nouveau witches such as the Gardnerians, most of whose rites have been published by Gerald B. Gardner in his books, and other newer Craft sects, such as the Alexandrians, who also use the Tarot in their rites, much as do the members of the Golden Dawn.

While on the subject of the Golden Dawn, one of the pupils of its one-time head, Samuel Mathers, was Aleister Crowley, who was initiated into the Hermetic Order of the Golden Dawn in November 1898. Until his death, one of the things that Crowley always had by him were the Tarot cards. He wrote a book on the subject called *The Book of Thoth*, which he published himself in 1944. Only 200 copies were printed. The cards depicted in this book were his own creation and were drawn by artist Frieda Harris. Crowley spent years working out this Tarot system. In his book *The Confessions of Aleister Crowley*, he writes:

> The true significance of the Atus of Tahuti, or Tarot Trumos, also awaits full understanding. I have satisfied myself that these twenty-two cards compose a complete system of hieroglyphs representing the total energies of the universe. In the case of some cards, I have succeeded in restoring the original form and giving a complete account of their meaning. Others, however, I understand imperfectly, and of some few I have at present obtained no more than a general idea.

Some of the most beautiful Tarot cards were originated in Italy. These include those by Baldini and Andrea Mategna; four ancient cards found in the Carrer Museum in Venice; the Minchiate or Florentine packs, which once belonged to the Countess Gonzaga of Milan (around 1413 to 1418); and the medieval Tarocchi deck still in use in the Piedmont area of Italy. The same popular games are played with them today as during the time of the Medicis and the Doges of Venice.

My own maternal grandmother and great-grandmother used the Tarot, and I paid brief tribute to them in my book *Curses in Verses: Spelltime in Rhyme.*

GRANDMAMA AND THE GYPSIES

Wandering Gypsies
    Spread Witchcraft lore
By sailing the seas
    Bringing Craft ashore
In Old Tuscany
    Whose Craft still survives
Came the Romany
    Enriching their lives
Exchanging their spells,
    And the herbal root
In time near church bells
    In Italy's boot.
They brought the Tarot
    Which my Nana read
Knowing tomorrow
    Summoning the dead
Grandmama strege
    A true Gypsy friend
Alpha and Omega
    Potions they would blend.

Two

Reading the Tarot Cards

The only way to read the Tarot cards is to just read them. Don't worry about whether or not you are psychic—you are. Everyone is psychic, but the psychic faculties of many people lie dormant and unused. Of course, some people are more psychic than others. To develop, release, and polish your psychic abilities requires *practice*. The greatest pianists in the world practice hours each day, because they realize that having a "gift" is not enough. The same holds true for psychic abilities.

Anyone can learn to play the piano, to paint, and to read Tarot cards. The difference between someone who is good at these things and someone who is not is the same. Two artists can possess all the tools of the trade—the same oils, brushes, canvas, and perhaps even the same teacher. Yet one produces a work of art and the other, a mediocre painting. The difference is that the *true* artist utilizes all the techniques but isn't restricted by them. The other type of artist paints according to the rules, and this automatically inhibits his imagination. The result of this is a painting that may be conventionally "nice" but is uninspiring. The work of the true artist may be disturbing, uplifting, depressing, or inspirational, but it is always *inspired*.

The same is true for a good reader of the Tarot. This type of reader knows all of the multiple meanings of the cards, has researched their ancient symbolism, and has an affinity with the cards. He realizes that the cards aren't just a means of telling the future. They are keys that can unlock the doors to insight, wisdom, and understanding. The intuition and intellect of the good reader are synchronized.

The incompetent reader of the Tarot depends solely upon the literal meanings of the cards and lacks psychic flexibility. The good reader uses the cards as a means toward an end, but not as an end in themselves. For the good reader, the cards are door openers and idea starters, and the accuracy of a reading depends upon the ability and experience of the reader. A reader with a totally negative attitude will not get full value out of a reading because he or she sets up a psychic block that will inhibit the spontaneity necessary for a good reading.

You cannot offer more than the sum total of your own knowledge and experience to the person being read. If you're limited in your psychological awareness of human motivations, you will only be able to touch upon superficial aspects of a problem, and offer cliché solutions. Also, if you assume that, deep down, the person really wants exactly what she says she does, you will be thrown off course. For example, there are many single women who go to various readers wishing to hear that they will meet the "right man." As I told one of them, "Do you know what will happen when you do? He'll be looking for the right woman! How do you know you will be that woman?"

The reader has to be able to read with a great deal of intuition and psychological insight. For example, another common occurrence is the woman who is involved with a married man and who tells the reader that she wishes he would get a divorce. But actually, when he does, she will no longer be interested! What sustains her interest in him is the fact that he is married—perhaps it is an unconscious way of "stealing daddy from mommy." Such women feel safe with a married man, and their "unhappiness" is a defense against their guilt over having exactly what they want. A superficial reader may merely tell her that she will or will not get her wish and not get to the heart of the reading because he or she has so little insight.

One question that is often asked is "Why is it that some Tarot readers are so accurate and others don't seem to know what they're talking about?" The answer is another question: Why is it that some writers are so moving and others so dull? Or that some music so soul-reaching and some just a conglomeration of sounds? Ability varies with different readers. The cards are the same, true, but the interpreters are not. We all use the very same words, but we can't all write bestsellers!

Tarot cards can be a wonderful channel for guidance, direction, truth, encouragement, and hope. They can be a psychological uplift, a mental stimulant, and even a spiritual outlet. A good Tarot reading can provide self-insight, give one confidence, and point out possible pitfalls. It can pave the way for a more positive attitude toward self, others, and life. But these readings should not be used as a substitute for individual effort, a false positive by someone not willing to back up wishes with work.

TAROT TABOOS

There are some things that should *not* be predicted when reading the Tarot—call them Tarot taboos. You should never predict death for the person being read or for close relatives of that person, and never predict serious illness. Things are always subject to change, and you are not infallible. Why cause unnecessary fear and worry? Besides, the deeper meaning of the Death Card means rebirth, renewal, or rejuvenation, the end of one thing and the beginning of another. You can always get around these dire predictions by asking questions like "When was the last time you visited the doctor?" or "I see death, but it's not someone close to you."

COLOR SYMBOLISM IN THE CARDS

Besides picture symbolism, which is explained in detail in this book, you should also be aware that the colors used in the cards are also symbolic. Generally, the red and black used in the cards are the colors of life and death, good and bad, day and night, hot and cold, summer and winter, light and dark, ego and id, consciousness and unconsciousness, and heaven and hell. These colors also stand for the colors of *Ra*, the Egyptian god of day, and *Set*, the Egyptian god of night, the underworld, and the nether regions. What feelings does the color red provoke in you? It probably makes you think of warmth, passion, love, comfort, vitality, fire, light, security, success, sex, and sensuality. It may also provoke such thoughts as anger, temper, and hostility. The negative associations with red concern *results*, but the causes are always *black*—I see red only when I'm provoked by a black deed.

Using the same free association, black represents, death, illness, fear, tragedy, accidents, the unconscious, the libido, worry, suffering, regrets, losses, resentment, mistakes, failure, depression, and the unknown. When we are depressed, or when the future looks bleak, we say that "everything looks black." Someone who is evil is "black-hearted." Trouble comes in "dark clouds." Black cards may indicate hurdles, problems, insecurity, enemies, opposition, tensions, neurosis, theft, threats, and fear of the unknown.

Before you start to read the Tarot cards, you should get a notebook and write down all the impressions you can think of associated with the colors red and black. Use the above as a starting point.

NUMBER SYMBOLISM

You should also make a separate listing for all the things you can think of associated with the numbered cards in the Minor Arcana. To help you begin, here is a partial number symbolism list.

I

One may symbolize any ace card, God, Goddess, ego, I, the first, a start, ace high, number one, the letter A (alpha in Greek, aleph in Hebrew), one world, alone, lonely, by oneself, January, Aries.

II

Two may symbolize the letter B, a pair, doubles, two of a kind, deuces wild, bicycle built for two, takes two to tango, Taurus, Monday, two-way stretch, tea for two, stand on your own two feet, two-timing, two sides to every story, two-faced, double-dealing, double agent, two of a kind, twins, ambivalence, bisexuality, duets.

III

Three may symbolize the Holy Trinity, triple threat, triangle, masculine sex symbol, letter C, three graces (faith, hope, and charity), three on a match, mystic three, Gemini, March, Tuesday, third party, two's company—three's a crowd, three wise men.

IV

Four may symbolize the four seasons, four corners of the earth, letter D, Wednesday, Cancer, four walls, four wheels, four legs (desk, table), four Evangelists (Matthew, Mark, Luke, and John), four elements (earth, air, fire, water), four-legged animals (pets), quarterlies, quadrangle, quarters.

V

Five may symbolize pentagram, pentagon, star, letter E, Thursday, May, Leo, musical staff made up of five lines, hands and feet.

VI

Six may symbolize the letter F, June, Virgo, Star of David, the last day of creation in Genesis signifying the completion of a job well done.

In the Minor Arcana the Six of Swords shows a man rowing a woman and child in a ferryboat to the opposite shore. All backs are turned to us but they face the shore. On the boat in front of them are six swords standing upright. Reverse the number 6 and you get 9 . . . both look like a sword or lance or fencing weapon, from which is derived the meaning of "separation" in a reading.

VII

Seven may symbolize the letter G, Saturday, July, Libra. Genesis 2:2 says "And on the seventh day God finished his work which he had done and He rested on the seventh day and hallowed it. . . . " Thus seven means change, rest, recreation, a turning point, the beginning and end of cycles, "lucky seven." In medicine, it is well known that the cells in our body change every seven years. Seven days of the week, "seventh heaven," again in Genesis 41:17, the Pharoah narrates a dream to Joseph which has seven fat cows and seven lean cows, the latter eating the former. He also speaks of seven good ears of corn and seven withered ones, the latter again eating the former. Joseph interprets this dream to mean seven years of prosperity followed by seven years of famine.

VIII

Eight may symbolize the letter H, August, Scorpio. Eight is composed of two equal parts indicating harmony, balance, justice, the Libran scales, as above so below, made sideways the sign of infinity, the eight good persons preserved from the great Biblical flood (Noah and his wife, three sons and their wives . . . eight in all), eighty-eight keys on a piano.

IX

Nine may symbolize the letter I, September, Sagittarius, the highest single number, since all others are composed of one to nine plus zero. "A stitch in time saves nine." "A cat has nine lives." Nine is the only number that can be multiplied by any other digit and the result, added, comes out to nine. Examples: 2 × 9 = 18 (8 + 1 = 9); 3 × 9 = 27 (2 + 7 = 9); 4 × 9 = 36 (3 + 6 = 9). You can go as high as you want and you will still get 9.

X

Ten may symbolize the letter J, October, Capricorn, in the Major Arcana the Wheel of Fortune . . . a completed cycle, thus the start of new one. The wheel symbolizes progress, travel, evolvement, a turning point. Negatively suggests going around in circles, in a spin, caught in a whirlpool, on a merry-go-round. It also denotes anything that revolves such as a merry-go-round, ferris wheel, roulette *chemin de fer*, or turntable. The Ten Commandments. The highest rating given to an attractive man or woman.

XI

Eleven may symbolize the letter K, November, Aquarius; in Numerology 11/22 is considered a Master Number. Symbolically, a person who rises above circumstances through sheer will (10 is Wheel of Fortune and One represents Self). The Knave is the eleventh card.

XII

Twelve may symbolize the letter L, December, Pisces, noon or midnight, the twelve months, the twelve apostles, the twelve signs of the Zodiac, the twelve tribes of Israel. The Queen is the twelfth card.

XIII

Thirteen may symbolize the letter M, Friday the 13th superstition, fear of the unknown. There were twelve apostles at the Last Supper plus Jesus. Witchcraft covens traditionally are made up of thirteen members. Many modern buildings omit the thirteenth floor, calling it either the fourteenth or 12A, based on the fear that this number is unlucky. In the Major Arcana it is the Death card. The King is the thirteenth card.

THE SIGNIFICANCE OF SURROUNDING CARDS

In a Tarot layout, all cards affect and are affected by surrounding cards. They have to be evaluated in relation to each other. Simply put, if most of the cards are black, or have negative connotations, the results don't look good. The reverse is true if most of the cards are red. If the last card is red and is preceded by mostly black cards, then the person has to overcome tremendous obstacles but will triumph in the end. If the last card is black and is preceded by mostly red cards, then the reading is mostly favorable, but there is some disappointment connected to the wish. Obviously, if the last few cards picked are black, this reveals disappointment. Common sense will show you how these various combinations represent what they do.

Many of the cards have more than one meaning, so all the surrounding cards, the person being read, and your own intuition determine which one is correct. Familiarize yourself with the Tarot cards. Keep a Tarot journal and write down any thoughts, impressions, and sayings associated with the specific meanings of each card, numbers, and colors. Practice reading them on friends or acquaintances. This will help you to "get into the groove," give you needed practice. As the Chinese proverb states, "A thousand mile journey begins with the first step."

Three

The Tarot Layout

There are many ways in which you can lay out the Tarot cards for a reading. However, before you begin, it's essential that you memorize the meanings of all the cards. These meanings are explained in Sections 4 and 5.

After you become proficient, you needn't be restricted by these meanings. Your subconscious mind (which we also call intuition) will detect subtleties and produce ideas and meanings that you should verbalize. Intuitive insight springs from a technical foundation, but more important than cut-and-dried facts is having a "feel" for the cards. This "feel" results in what I term "soul readings"—those that get to the essence of the person being read, to the heart of the matter: the true self as opposed to the "image" one presents. Some say that the cards must be shuffled a certain way, or that friendly "spirits" or "feelings" should be conjured up before a reading. This is not necessary. The success of the reading depends on the psychic abilities of the reader—that's all.

Each layout of cards is different for each person being read. One type of layout may work very well for one person, and poorly for another. This is where common sense and intuition are necessary. The symbolism is the same, and the reading will generally indicate whether the card represents something positive or negative, but the interpretation must be applied to the individual's own lifestyle. A row of Pentacles will represent freedom from financial worry for the hard-working man or woman and making a killing in the stock market for the business tycoon. And, the goals of a housewife are quite different from those of a career woman.

Before you begin the reading, remove the card that most nearly represents the person being read. Different authors give different interpretations of the colorings that are represented by the figure cards. I've found that the following works best for me:

King, Queen, Knight, and Page of Pentacles: Very fair; blond to light brown hair; blue, gray, or green eyes.

King, Queen, Knight, and Page of Swords: Very dark person; brown to black hair; brown or black eyes.

King, Queen, Knight, and Page of Cups: Medium coloring; usually blue, gray, or green eyes; from sandy to medium brown hair.

King, Queen, Knight, and Page of Wands: Medium dark coloring; brown eyes; light to dark brown hair.

After you have removed this card, use it as a "base" for your layout.

SIMPLIFIED METHOD I

Shuffle the deck of cards and cut it into three piles. You can either pick up the pile of cards on the left or spread the cards and have your subject select twenty-one. Place these cards face down as in Figure 3.1.

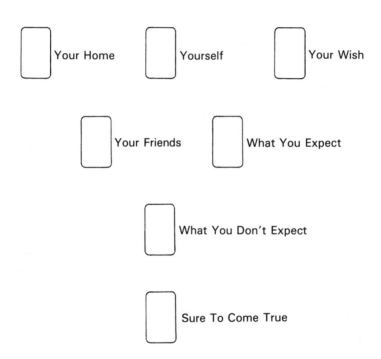

Figure 3.1. Simplified Method I.

Cover each one of these with three cards, placed face down. Then begin your reading. In using this method, some remove all the Tarot cards below the number seven, with the exception of the Aces, before shuffling the deck. The choice is yours.

THE ANCIENT CELTIC METHOD

An old method of Tarot layout, outlined in Waite's book, is the Ancient Celtic Method. Shuffle the cards and cut them into three packs. Have the subject pick the pack to use.

The easiest way to lay out the cards in the Celtic Method is to form them into a cross as shown in Figure 3.2.

With the picture card representing the subject in the center, you place the first card (1) directly on him and say, "This covers him/her."

Place the second card (2) right on top of that and say: "This crosses him."

Put the third card (3) directly above him and say, "This crowns him."

Place the fourth card (4) directly below (beneath) him and say, "This is beneath him."

Place the fifth card (5) to his left and say, "This is behind him."

Place the sixth card (6) to his right and say, "This is before him."

Starting with the seventh card, lay out cards seven through ten in a straight line, starting with seven at the bottom and ending with ten at the top, as in Figure 3.2.

When you lay out the seventh card (7) say, "This is you."

When you lay out the eighth card (8) say, "This is your home."

As you place the ninth card (9) say, "This is what you fear or hope."

As you place the tenth card (10) say, "This is the outcome."

After these cards are read, have the subject withdraw seven more cards. These are to add more depth to the reading and to answer any two questions the subject has. For a more detailed and varied reading you can place three cards in each of the enumerated positions outlined above.

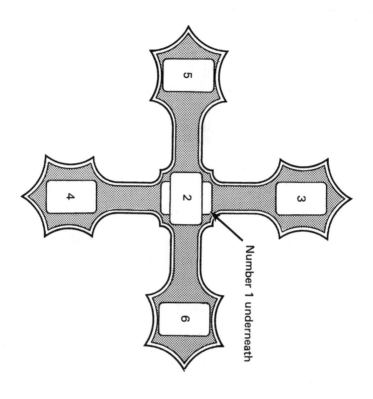

Number 1 underneath

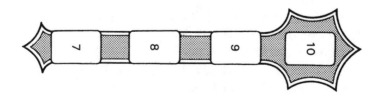

Figure 3.2. The Ancient Celtic Method.

THE WHEEL OF FORTUNE

In this method, you can use all of the Tarot cards or remove all the cards below the seven except the Aces. Again, select the card that represents the coloring of the person being read (Queen of Cups, King of Wands, etc.). This card is to be placed in the center of the wheel. After the cards are shuffled, cut them into three packs after the questioner has made his wish. Begin to lay out the Wheel of Fortune as in Figure 3.3. Do this in the following manner:

The card representing the person is to be placed at the center of the wheel.

1. Place the first card above the person.

2. Place the second card below the person.

3. Place the third card to the right of the person.

4. Place the fourth card to the left of the person.

5. Place the fifth card between the first and third cards.

6. Place the sixth card between the second and third cards.

7. Place the seventh card between the second and fourth cards.

8. Place the eighth card between the fourth and first cards.

As shown in Figure 3.3, the first four cards form a cross while the next four are laid out diagonally, in between the spokes of the cross and forming an X. This layout is the nucleus of the Wheel of Fortune.

After you have laid out the cards as in Figure 3.3, lay out the remaining cards, starting at the top of the first card and working clockwise until all are laid out in a full circle. This circle is your Wheel of Fortune—it will have eight spokes. The last card should end up on the right side

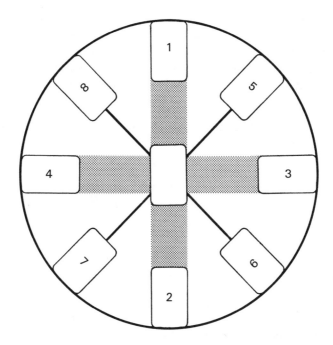

Figure 3.3.   The Wheel of Fortune.

of your subject in the row that began with the third card (number 3 above).

To begin reading the cards, follow either of the following methods.

Since the subject is the "center of his own universe," begin reading the cards from the center outwards. How a row ends will determine whether the outcome is good or bad.

Or, begin to read each spoke in the Wheel of Fortune. You can either begin at the top and work your way around the circle or begin wherever you wish—whatever "hits" you first.

Generally, the Wheel of Fortune is read as follows:

- The cards on the row or spoke on the left side of the wheel and beneath the wheel represent what is past, or what the subject's subconscious desires are.

- The cards below the person represent what the person is stepping on.

- The cards above in the first spoke directly above the face card and to the right of the person represent the future, or "what's on your mind"—what you hope for.

This follows the ancient traditional thought that what is to the right is ahead of us, in the future, and what is to the left is associated with the past, what is behind us.

The cards can also be read as the subject's conscious and subconscious desires—"what's on your mind." The cards directly above and to the right of the card in the center represent conscious hopes, wishes, goals, desires, and feelings. The subconscious is represented by the rows directly to the left and especially beneath the person. Very often, what is depicted in the conscious and subconscious rows is incompatible or reveals conflict. This is because a person may unconsciously want something, yet be held back by subconscious doubts, fears, or uncertainties. There may be a moral dilemma involved.

For example, a woman may be offered marriage to a man who can give her security. She may be tempted by the security, yet hesitate because she is not in love with the man. Another example is someone who consciously wants to change his job, but hesitates, because he lacks confidence, feels insecure, or isn't sure whether it's a wise move.

When you sense this, check the rows, and if they're predominantly made up of Cups, Pentacles, and Wands, the only correct answer is, "The doubt exists in your mind, but there is none in your cards." You can't discount the person's fears, so talk about it and bring it into the open. Point out that the Tarot reflects the outer reality, the possibility of attainment, and that any negativity or doubt felt may postpone things or make them more difficult, but doesn't negate them.

THE NEXT TWELVE MONTHS

In this method, you lay out all the Tarot cards into twelve piles representing the twelve months, as in Figure 3.4. Since there are seventy-eight Tarot cards, the first six piles will have seven cards each, and the last six piles, six cards each.

In laying out the Tarot in this method, do so one by one—first card on January, second on February, third on March, etc. Continue to do this in rotation until all the cards are laid out. After this, pick up the first pile and read them for January, and continue to do so with each month.

January 7	February 7	March 7	April 7	May 7	June 7
July 6	August 6	September 6	October 6	November 6	December 6

Figure 3.4. The Next Twelve Months.

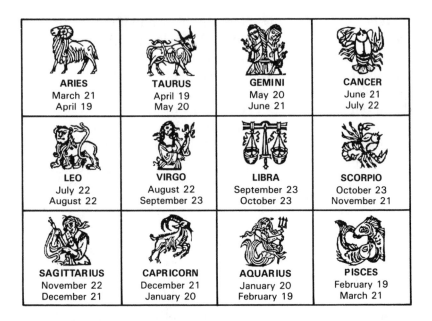

ARIES March 21 April 19	**TAURUS** April 19 May 20	**GEMINI** May 20 June 21	**CANCER** June 21 July 22
LEO July 22 August 22	**VIRGO** August 22 September 23	**LIBRA** September 23 October 23	**SCORPIO** October 23 November 21
SAGITTARIUS November 22 December 21	**CAPRICORN** December 21 January 20	**AQUARIUS** January 20 February 19	**PISCES** February 19 March 21

Figure 3.5.   The Astrological Layout.

THE ASTROLOGICAL TAROT

Lay out the Tarot as enumerated in Figure 3.5, covering the zodiacal months, and read accordingly. You can also read about someone whose birth date falls within each sign. Examples: "Someone born under the sign of Leo came close to death as a child" or "Someone under the sign of Scorpio resents you very much" or "Someone close to you born under Libra had a broken marriage," etc. If the Nine of Cups falls in the Aquarius layout surrounded by Cups, Wands, or Pentacles and no Swords, that's the period indicated for the realization of the person's wish . . . or at least it indicates the beginning of the fulfillment, when things start to happen, when the subject will have some concrete evidence of it. If surrounded entirely by Swords, it means the subject won't get his wish.

SIMPLIFIED METHOD II

Another simplified method is to read the middle pile of cards after the Tarot has been cut into three as in Figure 3.6. Just lay them out side by side and read them in relation to each other. Then have the subject pick cards from one of the piles. He will ask the reader questions about his life, and, based on the cards, the reader will answer them.

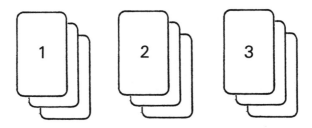

Figure 3.6.   Simplified Method II.

Four

The Major Arcana

The twenty-two cards of the Major Arcana of the Tarot have occupied the minds of intellectuals, occultists, philosophers, mystics, and parapsychologists ever since they have been in existence. Psychologists have recognized their universal symbolism. Each card can trigger a person's subconscious, setting off impressions, images, thoughts, and associations. Involved with such matters as life and death, good and evil, love and hate, strength and folly, success and failure, truth and falsehood, their symbols cover the whole of human experience. The cards are called keys because they unlock doors to knowledge and symbolism and give insight into the future.

Many read only the Major Arcana, and not so much to "know the future" but as a means of philosophical-psychological insight, as a guide similar to the *I Ching*. The collective unconscious theory of psychoanalyst C. G. Jung explains the Tarot symbols as universal archetypes existing in the minds of all peoples. P. D. Ouspensky has delved into the Tarot occult traditions in his *A New Model of the Universe*. Poet W. B. Yeats was a member of the Order of the Golden Dawn and poet T. S. Eliot's *The Waste Land* touches on the Tarot.

Because the book is written for the new student of the Tarot, I haven't included the Tree of Life reading—this method of reading should only be undertaken by the advanced student who has a full knowledge of the Cabala. Those who are interested in using the Tarot for divination have more than enough information here to go on.

The Fool

DESCRIPTION   KEY 0

A young man approaches the edge of a cliff. His head is held high and he looks straight ahead, unaware or unafraid of danger. He carries a wand in his right hand with a pouch or purse at its end and a white rose in his left hand. The sun blazes overhead, a dog is at his heels, and mountains are in the background.

SYMBOLISM

Though this card is often placed at the end of the Tarot, it should be its start. Key 0 is the alpha and omega of existence. All or nothing at all. The innocent on life's pathway. He doesn't know which direction is right but he has the choice to succeed or fail, rise or fall. Wisdom comes from experience. He must make this journey. The white rose symbolizes his innocence (purity, virginity). With few possessions and a faithful dog who follows him blindly, he is bright with promise (the sun) and unaware of the pitfalls (the precipice). He begins as The Fool (0) and can end up worldly-wise (Key 21). In between, the next twelve cards depict his childhood, adolescence (The Hanged Man: Key 12), and maturity.

MEANING

You have a choice in life. No matter which path you choose, at the end of each life lies a destiny. Knowledge comes from trial and error. There are guideposts on life's journey but there are no guarantees. Whether you will end up a wise man or remain a fool depends upon the choices and the decisions that you make. Thus, this card in a reading means blind faith, foolishness, unwarranted optimism, errors of judgement, "you learn by your mistakes." Those who don't "live and learn" are doomed to repeat their mistakes.

REVERSED

You may have made a wrong decision. Check your premises, analyze your assumptions, re-evaluate your motives.

The Fool

The Magician

DESCRIPTION   KEY 1

Above The Magician's head is the Sign of Infinity, a horizontal
number eight. The table in front of him contains symbols of
the four suits: Sword, Wand, Pentacle, and Cup. His right
hand holds a wand pointing upwards (heaven). His left hand
is pointing downwards (earth, hell). He stands in a garden of
roses and lilies. His waist is encircled by a serpent devouring
its own tail.

SYMBOLISM

The four symbols represent the four elements: earth, air,
fire, and water. In some decks this figure is called the Juggler.
The secrets of the universe are contained within man himself.
He is able to tap all the resources and use them for his own
benefit. This mastery over the elements, self, and others is
acquired through occult knowledge, psychic power, and full
use of the mind. We all have free will and can carve out of the
rock of life our own Fate through study, work, and application. The self-consuming serpent is another symbol of eter-
nity.

MEANING

Self-mastery, self-direction, self-control, self-sustenance. One
who is "his own man (or woman)." The conscious application
of will directed toward achievement, yet utilizing unconscious
factors. The ability to program oneself for success, positive
thinking, to "make things happen." This requires intelligence,
initiative, self-confidence, and a self-sustaining ego, one not
dependent upon the approval, opinions, or suggestions of
others. This is not the defensive "ego" in popular parlance
(which is really a self-protective mask for insecurity) but that
ego which is of supreme self-confidence (and, for the spiritual
minded, that ego which identifies itself with God).

REVERSED

Cunning, deceit, charlatanry, exploitation, twisting things
and words around to suit one's own purposes.

The Magician

The High Priestess

DESCRIPTION   KEY 2

This figure is sometimes called the Papess or Pope Joan. She sits on a throne with a crescent moon at her feet and a cross on her breast, between two pillars, one black with the letter *B*, the other white with the letter *J*. The scroll on her lap is the Torah, meaning the Greater or Secret Law. This is partly hidden by her mantle. She wears the horned diadem on her head. The veil behind her is covered with pomegranates and palms.

SYMBOLISM

The black pillar is Boaz, the negative life principle. The white one is Jakin, the positive life principle. (These are the names of pillars in front of Solomon's temple.) The partly hidden Torah scroll means hidden knowledge, veiled mysteries, subconscious power, an enigma, the secret self, occult science. The veil is decorated with palms, which symbolize the male, and pomegranates, which symbolize the female. The headdress of a diadem, a crescent moon, also forming horns, is very significant to practitioners of the Old Religion of Witchcraft. They worship both a Horned God and a Goddess. She is the Supernal Mother, the hidden church, the Moon Goddess, the Cabalistic *Shekinah*, and this card is considered by most adepts to be the highest and the holiest in the Major Arcana.

MEANING

Subconscious knowledge, intuition, inspiration, occult wisdom, hidden mysteries, tapping one's inner resources, the power of the subconscious mind to effect change and healing in one's own life, the ability to get to one's own inner center and function as an effective, creative, life-affirming human being.

REVERSED

A superficial, shallow person; a "plastic personality"; one who lacks depth; one lacking in subtlety, insight, and perceptiveness; external knowledge.

The High Priestess

The Empress

KEY 3

DESCRIPTION

A regal woman is seated, wearing a crown of twelve stars. By her side is a heart-shaped shield bearing the sign of Venus. In her right hand she holds a scepter, ending in the world-globe. In front of her there is a ripe field of corn, to her left a waterfall or stream, and in back of her trees in full bloom.

SYMBOLISM

The Earth Mother, symbolizing fertility, growth, harvest, abundance, productiveness. She is Isis, whom the Egyptians believed the mother-goddess of generation. She is Venus-Astarte-Aphrodite, goddess of human love, and also Hermaphrodite, wherein both sexes are united into one person. The Hermetics and many ancients believe this to be the perfect nature of the Creator.

MEANING

The Empress means abundance in all human affairs, healthy children for parents who desire them, good crops for farmers and agriculturists, big profits for businessmen and industrialists, a rich reservoir of ideas for the creative artist. The number three is a universal sex symbol and denotes the fulfillment of one's erotic needs. In the occult the meaning is nonsexual, but signifies the union of the male and female, positive and negative, yin and yang principles. She represents "heaven on earth," the "Garden of Eden," the door that open unto earthly pleasures and treasures, while The High Priestess represents the cosmic subconscious, the deeper inner mysteries.

REVERSED

Dissipation, wastefulness, poverty, frustration, failure, destruction, disunity, unproductiveness, lack of growth, bankrupt ideas.

The Empress

The Emperor

KEY 4

DESCRIPTION

Regal, authoritative, patriarchal, he sits on a throne, the armrests and upper side made into rams' heads. In his left hand he holds the globe, in his right, the Cross of Life, the Egyptian Ankh. On his right shoulder there is another image of the ram's head. Behind him are stark mountains, devoid of any scenery.

SYMBOLISM

The Emperor is ruler of the intellect, conscious thought, earthly knowledge. He is concerned with government, affairs of the state, politics, ruled by his mind rather than his emotions. The stark mountains and his own stern regal posture indicate uncompromising virtue. He is preoccupied with the letter of law and order, unyielding in his temporal power, unbending in his judgements. Waite calls him the "lord of thought rather than of the animal world."

MEANING

Intellectual pursuits, interests, goals. Reason dominating passion. Mind over matter. Fully developed conscious intelligence rather than depending upon instincts. The leader rather than the follower. The archetype of Osiris, husband-brother of Isis (the Empress), worldly-wise, practical, pragmatic. He represents leadership, being in command, power, authority, a high position in life, strength, "getting to the top," executive ability, political prowess, self-discipline, one who "rules with an iron hand."

REVERSED

Lack of self-discipline, dependency, no direction in life, threat to one's authority, irrationality. Secret plots, attempts to usurp one's power or property.

The Emperor

The Hierophant

KEY 5

DESCRIPTION

Sometimes called the Pope, he sits between two pillars wearing the triple crown. His left hand upholds the triple cross while his right hand forms the ecclesiastical sign of esotericism. There are two crossed keys at his feet. Before him kneel two initiates or subject priests.

SYMBOLISM

He represents organized religion and all the temporal power and ritual that goes with it. Structured, dogmatic, orthodox, organized, the outer church, The Hierophant is the symbol of conventional religious conduct, unquestioned acceptance of childhood-taught beliefs, blind faith, the rigid theologian rather than the questing and questioning philosopher. While The High Priestess communicates only with the initiated, The Hierophant speaks to the multitudes.

MEANING

Conventional conduct, conformity, adherence to the outer forms of religion and social conduct (the regular churchgoer who does so out of habit), those who prefer all the surface trappings of religion rather than any deep understanding of the inner mysteries, plastic personalities engaged in pomp and ceremony. The Hierophant stands for the search for truth but is not himself "The Truth." Also symbolical of the Establishment, the system, status-quo, "that's the way it has always been done."

REVERSED

Unconventional, original, daring, unorthodox, even revolutionary. One who is receptive to new ideas, willing to challenge authority or tradition, not bound by dogma, public opinion, or fear of disapproval.

The Lovers

The Chariot

KEY 7

DESCRIPTION

A proud, princely figure rides a chariot, in front of which lie
two sphinxes. The left one is black, the right one is white.
The figure carries a wand in his right hand. On his shoulders
are the figures of Urim and Thummim. On the forefront of
The Chariot is the Indian *ligam* on top of which is the flying
sphere of the Egyptians.

SYMBOLISM

This figure represents conquest, external gain, self-mastery,
the union of the good and bad (white and black), sensuality
(lingam), and spirituality (winged sphere). He needs to exercise his willpower at all times to keep these divergent elements
balanced so that neither sphinx shall take possession or try
to run off in different directions at once (conflicting ideas,
desires, thoughts, etc.).

MEANING

Self-possession, willpower, mastery of self, man's mind as his
only weapon for survival, a full conscious awareness of what
is good and what is evil, what is beneficial and what is destructive. A hedonist is not master of himself, but a slave to his
desires. Achievement is possible only to those who exercise
self-discipline. Others fall by the wayside. Triumph, victory,
honors, achievement. Life can't be all play and no work. Nor
can it be all work and no play. Harnessing one's energies and
talents constructively.

REVERSED

Dissipation of energies, talents, self-indulgence, hedonism. A
phony or false triumph, an unearned reward, pretentious
honors, a scandal, notoriety, graft, "things caving in."

The Chariot

Strength

KEY 8

DESCRIPTION

A woman with the sign of Infinity over her head is bending over and closing the jaws of a lion. Around her waist and encircling the lion's neck is a garland of flowers. The Rider deck prepared for Arthur Edward Waite and designed by Pamela Coleman Smith (used in this book) transposed Keys 8 and 11, making the first *Strength* and the latter *Justice*. Waite wrote in his *Pictorial Key to the Tarot*: "For reasons which satisfy myself, this card has been interchanged with that of Justice, which is usually numbered eight." For many modern Tarot readers this is arbitrary. Eight symbolizes equidistance, as above, so below, the Libran scales of balance, from which is derived justice.

SYMBOLISM

In gentleness lies true strength. You see this demonstrated by the gentleness of big men, fighters, intellectual giants, scientific geniuses, etc. On the other hand is the vindictiveness of little men who try to dominate by threats, force, deception, and tyranny. I'm speaking here of "big" and "little" as character descriptions, not necessarily physical dimensions.

MEANING

Overcome obstacles, intestinal fortitude, spiritual power stronger than material power, passions subdued, quiet determination, sweet reason over roaring irrationality, exemplified in the saying, "You can catch more flies with honey than vinegar."

REVERSED

Disharmony, abuse of power, tyranny, attempt to use force to gain one's ends, dictatorial, chauvinistic, domineering, lacking self-control.

Strength

The Hermit

KEY 9

DESCRIPTION

A lonely figure is atop a snow-covered mountain peak looking down on the people and country below. He carries an uplifted lantern in his right hand. In his left hand he holds a staff or wand. There is a bright shining star inside the Lantern.

SYMBOLISM

Every person must find his own way and his own truth. The search for self, for identity, for self-esteem is often a lonely one. We are all alone within the sanctuary of our minds. Others can't give us our sense of value, nor can they take it away if we have it. While The Fool is a young man looking upwards to the morning light, The Hermit gazes into the darkness of night. This card reminds me of the saying: "All the darkness in the world cannot hide the light of the littlest candle."

MEANING

"Seek and ye shall find. Knock and the door shall be opened unto you." The star-lit lantern is a projection of inner illumination, meditation, contemplation. The hermit symbolizes all the holy men of history, from Christ to Buddha, enlightened, lonely, sad sages . . . sad at the insight into human folly, but not bitter. Wise in the ways of man. Can represent a guide, a guru, a counselor, wisdom, insight, enlightenment, understanding. "Help along the way," but the responsibility for your life is ultimately yours.

REVERSED

Isolation, alienation, lack of communication with others, loneliness, abandonment, emotional and spiritual deprivation. Persistence in bad habits. The person who tries to stay young disgracefully rather than to grow old gracefully.

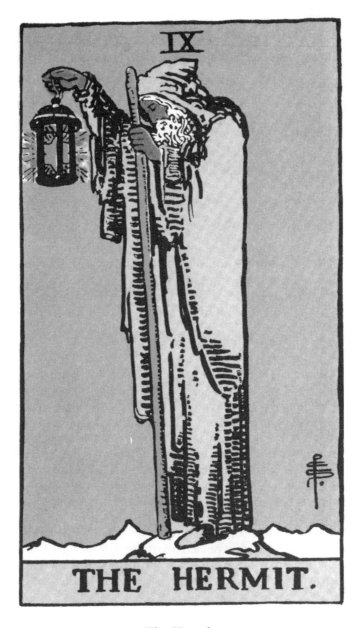

The Hermit

Wheel of Fortune

DESCRIPTION   KEY 10

The four corners of this card depict the Four Living Creatures of Ezekiel. Sitting on top of the Wheel is a Sphinx. Reading clockwise, the wheel spells out the word Taro. Interspersed are the Hebrew letters of IHVH (Jod-He-Vau-He) or Jehovah or God. The left side of the wheel has a serpent. The right side depicts Hermes-Anubis, the Egyptian jackal-headed god. All the creatures have wings.

SYMBOLISM

The upper left depicts an angel, Aquarius; the upper right, an eagle, Scorpio. The lower left is a winged bull, Taurus. The lower right is a winged lion, Leo. These correspond to the fixed signs of the zodiac. Inside the wheel are the signs for mercury (on top), sulphur (right), salt (left), and water (Aquarius) below.

MEANING

The discovery of the wheel is considered the beginning of civilization, leading to travel, progress, and growth. Life itself is a gamble. This card denotes "the turn of events" in one's life. It constantly turns, from top to bottom, then to top again, from elation to despair to elation. Everything passes. The only constant thing in life is change. Things taking a turn for the better . . . making progress in one's life, work, goals. Getting ahead. Being in the driver's seat . . . in control of one's life, destiny, luck. The wheel, or circle, signifies completion, a job well done, tasks finished. Life itself is not a straight line upwards, and this card inherently has to do with fate, luck, fatality, the unexpected twists and turns. But it also implies that man always has the steering wheel of his own mind to rise above adversity. The wheel turns, life goes on.

REVERSED

Stagnancy, a turn for the worse, things at a standstill, topsy-turvy conditions.

Wheel of Fortune

Justice

KEY 11

DESCRIPTION

A woman sits on a throne between two pillars. Behind her is a veil. She holds a sword in her upraised right hand. In her left she holds the Scales of Justice and Balance. She's wearing a crown with three turrets with a square jewel in its center. She is *not* blindfolded.

SYMBOLISM

The double-edge sword, symbolic of Justice being a "two-way street . . . what's good for you is good for me." For the correct numerical evaluation of this card, see Key 8: Strength (they should be transposed). Unlike modern depictions of Justice, her eyes are *open*. Justice is *not* blind, which would be a contradiction in terms.

MEANING

Justice, fair play, equilibrium, a balanced life. One who weighs his words and actions, considers both sides of a story, and tries to get all the facts. Only then is he in a position to make a judgement, form a conclusion, arrive at a decision. Identified with the Goddess Themis, adviser to the gods. Implies the Law of Karma: "As ye sow so shall ye reap." Also, "Do unto others as you would want them to do unto you." Justice is severe, impartial, objective, detached, uninfluenced by any consideration except what is right and what is wrong.

REVERSED

Injustice, legal delays and setbacks, excesses in drink, sex, materialism, overindulgence. Bias, bigotry, prejudice, chauvinism, racism, victimization, unfair judgements, penalties, sentences.

Justice

The Hanged Man

DESCRIPTION

KEY 12

A young man is suspended upside down on a T-cross made
of living wood. His legs form a cross. His face, though, is
beatific, and there's a halo around his head. The top part of
the *tau* (T) tree has growing leaves. His arms are folded behind
his back.

SYMBOLISM

St. Peter was hanged upside down by the Romans. There is
nothing in this card that shows suffering. Rather, it indicates
that kind of sacrifice or martyrdom indulged in by holy men
and saints, those who died joyfully for a cause. The head and
folded arms form an inverted triangle . . . the Cabalistic sign
of water. His legs form a cross. The whole symbolism of this
card expresses life, not death; entrancement, not pain; joy,
not sorrow. Its symbolism is subtle.

MEANING

Note that there is nothing here to show that The Hanged Man
is even tied (let alone nailed) to the cross. He is literally standing on his head. This has humorous and philosophical connotations, such as surrender of self to a Higher Authority; "shak-
ing up one's brains," or turning oneself inside out or upside
down to effect a change; letting the blood run to the head
in order to revitalize one's mind. Suspended judgement, post-
poned plans, the need to "shake oneself up" and make some
sacrifices in order to achieve desired goals, reversing the direction of one's life. There is an implication of bondage here,
and the further implication that one can free oneself as well.

REVERSED

Pretensions in being "upright." A false prophet. Absorption
in mundane matters to the exclusion of subtle (spiritual) influences. One requiring a prop to his ego, chained to material
concepts and matters.

The Hanged Man

Death

KEY 13
DESCRIPTION

Depicted as a white skeleton dressed in black, on a white
horse, slowly moving across a field. He carries a black banner
emblazoned with the mystic white rose, its inner and outer
petals forming two pentagrams. The sun shines on the horizon
between two towers. A dead body lies in his path while he is
being awaited by a priest with clasped hands, a maiden, and
a child. The dead body is that of a king.

SYMBOLISM

While The Hanged Man is subtle and mystical, this card has
both mystical and immediate significance. This is the thirteenth card. He is the Grim Reaper, the destiny that awaits
us all: Death, a fate no one can escape. But this doesn't necessarily mean physical death. It can mean the end of one kind
of life, the beginning of a new one (rehabilitated alcoholics,
drug addicts, criminals, etc.). Before one can be reborn, phys-
ically, spiritually or psychologically, he must first die.

MEANING

Could mean a physical death, a transformation, reincarnation,
rebirth, change in the course of one's life, consciousness rais-
ing, regeneration, "things get worse before they get better"
(like undergoing and recovering from a major operation).
The Lord of the Gates, representing light and darkness, day
and night, the thirteen lunar cycles, the end of one year, the
beginning of a new one. Though thirteen is often considered
unlucky (especially to Christians because at the Last Supper
there were thirteen present), it is not so in and of itself. And
the death is followed by resurrection.

REVERSED

Things at a standstill, stagnation, "deadbeat" and dull,
"nothing happening," neither life nor death—mere existence.

Death

Temperance

DESCRIPTION   KEY 14

An angel is pouring liquid, "the essences of life," from one
chalice into another. One foot is in the water, the other on
land. He wears the sun-sign on his head (circle with dot inside)
and on his breast is a square with a triangle enclosed. Above
this are the Hebrew letters IHVH . . . Jod He Vau He, the
sacred name of God. In the background the sun shines
brightly over two mountain peaks.

SYMBOLISM

A close study of this figure indicates that it is neither male
nor female. Thus, it represents union of the male and female
principle. It also symbolizes spirit entering matter, the fluid
life-force of the male fertilizing the life-seed of the female.
Following the Death card, Temperance implies the Resurrection . . . the Light after Dark. The Angel of Time, indicating
patience and harmony. Winter will pass and then the blossom-
ing of spring, the "stream of life," goes on.

MEANING

Use moderation in all you do, avoid extremes. You can exper-
iment and speculate and try new ventures. Don't hesitate to
"get your toes wet" as long as you keep one foot planted
firmly on the ground! It would be absurd for you to dive into
deep water if you can't swim! Take one step at a time and
you'll get there. This card implies organizational ability, man-
agement, the trying out of different combinations until you
hit upon the right one, measuring and mixing the ingredients
of life into happy-harmonious combinations.

REVERSED

False premises, wrong assumptions, "too many irons in the
fire," competing interests, professional, personal, or social
relations with people where there's a wrong chemistry;
impatience, in too much of a hurry.

Temperance

The Devil

DESCRIPTION   KEY 15

A horned devil dominates this card. He has bat-like wings
and sits on a small stool or symbolic altar. His right hand is
raised (the opposite of the upraised hand of the Hierophant
in Key 5) while in his left hand he holds a torch pointing
downwards. There is an inverted pentagram (star) on his
forehead. On his right side is a small figure of a naked woman,
on his left side one of a naked man. Around their necks are
chains which are linked from both ends to the altar, but the
chains are loose enough for them to remove. This card is the
direct opposite of The Lovers shown in Key 6.

SYMBOLISM

The evil-negative-dark side of life exemplified in the Persian
Ahriman, the Egyptian Seth, the Hebrew Apollyon, the Chris-
tian Satan. My own interpretation is that Hedonism is not
freedom to do whatever one wants but *slavery* to one's desires.
The chains around their necks are removable but dominated
by the idea that evil is power. They are prisoners of their own
premises.

MEANING

Self-indulgence, sensation, and sensuality without sense. The
tailed figures indicate animal-like conduct. They have the
freedom to break loose but don't know this or haven't utilized
it. Chained by materialistic values and believing they own
things when in reality they are owned by them. Their possessions possess them. A matter of believing that money makes
the man instead of man makes money. Someone practicing
malevolent magic, involved with Satanism, devil worship, hex-
ing, and the like. A warning of trouble from one's indulgences.

REVERSED

One beginning to see the light, a conscious effort to change
one's ways, to break away from bad influences, to eliminate
undesirable elements or people.

The Devil

The Tower

DESCRIPTION   KEY 16

A tower is struck by lightning, its crown blown off. Fire is coming out of its top and windows and there are twenty-two falling bits of light (which are Hebrew yods). There are two falling figures plunging to the rocky precipice below.

SYMBOLISM

This has also been called the House of God and the Tower of Destruction. The yods symbolize the life force descending unto the material world—spirit permeating matter. The lightning is from the same source as that of The Magician and in The Hermit's lantern. To get the proper interpretive feeling for this card, think in terms of the Fall of Man, the Tower of Babel, the banishment of angels from heaven, the "fall from grace," etc.

MEANING

Catastrophe, destruction, disruption, "the roof caved in." Bedlam and bankruptcy. Fall from power. Broken marriage, friendship, family, divorce. Homes, businesses, or other property destroyed by fire, earthquakes, tornadoes, floods, etc. Traditional mores and modes of life being overthrown. Tearing down of existing structures and dogmas. A person who is hit with one problem after another, as in the old saying, "It never rains, it pours." The tyrant who has risen to the top on the backs of others is toppled from his throne when those he has abused rise up against him. The destruction of false ideas, values, beliefs, doctrines, laws, and institutions, both secular and religious. Those who have built their power on phony or false foundations, who have literally erected a "house of cards," exist with the subconscious realization that it's only a matter of time before it falls apart.

REVERSED

This is still not good but the danger isn't as great as above. The threat is of lesser degree.

The Tower

The Star

DESCRIPTION   KEY 17

A naked woman kneels on her left knee on the ground. Her right foot is in the water. She is pouring water out of one vase into the pool of water, while her right hand is pouring water on land from another vase. Behind her is a star-shaped sun, with seven other smaller stars surrounding it, indicating the sun and seven planets. On her right side is a shrub, upon which sits a bird.

SYMBOLISM

The pouring of water symbolizes Life (spirit) while the earth represents matter. This card suggests Mother Nature, radiant youth, identified with The High Priestess and The Empress, and subtly with Key 14, Temperance. The shrub is analogous to the Tree of Life, while the bird symbolizes the soul—"free as a bird." In graphology, the doodling of stars indicates preoccupation with goals, aspirations, aims, hopes, and dreams. The water represents the "waters of life," which constantly replenish themselves, and the "gifts of the spirit," which is the attainment of worthy goals.

MEANING

Aspiration, hope, ambition, goals, guidance, direction, purpose in life, inner satisfaction, feeling of accomplishment, sense of achievement, courage, idealism (especially in the young), spiritual and psychological insight. "Wishing on a star" and "reaching for the stars" and "hitching your wagon to a star" kind of optimism. In a reading it means "getting your wish" and "achieving your goals." Whether these "high hopes" are valid or not depends upon surrounding cards.

REVERSED

Hopelessness, doubt, disillusionment, lack of perception, pessimism, one's hopes "dashed to the ground," and "brought down to earth with a bang."

The Star

The Moon

KEY 18

DESCRIPTION

A full moon with a face is shining down on a sleeping earth. Bits of light or "yods" fall from it. Two dogs and a crab in the water are the only signs of life. On each side of the card are two gray towers. A path ascends to the towers.

SYMBOLISM

The moon represents man's subconscious, while the falling yods are the life force. The wolf symbolizes man's untamed unconscious, the id, while the dog represents adaptation and adjustment to man. The crab symbolizes primitive awareness, the beginnings of conscious awareness. The dog's mistress is Diana, goddess of the chase, while the wolf and crab are more identified with Hecate, goddess of the "dark side of the moon."

MEANING

The word "lunatic" comes from the Latin word *luna*. In ancient times, it was believed that certain people became strangely and adversely affected by the moon and this is still believed today. The Moon represents the subconscious, instincts, feelings, dreams, sleeping side of man. It represents the unknown, mystic, mysterious, hidden, imaginative aspects of nature. It is the psychoanalytic id, the animal side of man and those things that are hidden and emerge at night. "A wolf in sheep's clothing." Imagination, intuition, the unforeseen, secret enemies, those urges that are usually suppressed or repressed.

REVERSED

To be in control of one's urges or a threatening situation. Harnessed energy instead of "letting your imagination run away with you." The ability to "keep peace" despite inner turmoil. Not permitting the tactics or attacks of enemies to make one lose control of judgement.

The Moon

The Sun

DESCRIPTION   KEY 19

A brightly burning sun with a benign face dominates the top part of this card. On the left side are three huge sunflowers. There is another one on the right. In the foreground, a naked child is riding a white horse without a saddle and is carrying a bright red banner.

SYMBOLISM

The sun rises in the East. The four sunflowers indicate that the four natural kingdoms (mineral, vegetable, animal, human) and the four elements (earth, air, fire, water) face the child. This means that it is up to man to harness them and make them work, grow, and produce. They wait to be cultivated. The child's nakedness represents innocence, purity, a guilt-free spirit.

MEANING

The sun has always been linked with gold, thus, "A golden opportunity." It means attainment, success, growth, material wealth, personal satisfaction, a "sunny disposition," things "bright with promise," good luck, a "lucky break." If this follows a series of negative cards, it means that despite all the obstacles and trouble the final result is favorable . . . the "darkness before the dawn." After the storm the rainbow. The sun is the most important life-sustaining element on earth, concerns the here and now. In a reading requiring a "yes" or "no" answer, The Sun always means "yes." It is clarity, conscious awareness, "things out in the open," joy, and happiness.

REVERSED

"All that glitters is not gold." False hope, irrational optimism, unfounded plans, involvements and pursuits based on a temporary "ignorance is bliss" state, reverses in one's life, plans, relationships. The Sun reversed has inherent good fortune but is subject to re-evaluation. The need for a more realistic "down to earth" approach.

The Sun

Judgement

DESCRIPTION   KEY 20

The Archangel Gabriel is blowing his horn, encompassed by but rising above clouds, with a banner that has a cross in its center. The banner is attached to the trumpet. In the foreground the dead are rising from their coffins with outstretched arms towards Gabriel. In the distance there are stark mountains.

SYMBOLISM

The naked man, woman, and child in the foreground indicate consciousness, the subconscious, and regeneration, respectively. Judgement Day. Karmic debt. "As ye sow so shall ye reap." Rebirth, regeneration, and resurrection. Life after death. Day of Atonement. Eternal life. Death itself is merely a long sleep, leading from one life to the next.

MEANING

Atonement, "Your day will come." Symbolizes rebirth, a renewal of the spirit, a "second chance." You can refuse to know something but you cannot escape the consequences of your refusal. Simply, this card means "coming to your senses," discarding whims and "feelings" as tools of knowledge, and exercising your mind in order to make correct judgements. A warning to be more prudent. The need to take a long hard look at yourself and ask: Why am I here? What am I doing? Where am I going? What is the purpose of my life? Making a change based on a careful analysis of the total situation. A new life-style. Freeing oneself from the tombs of habit and sameness, becoming "alive" once more, breaking out of a rut (tomb, coffin, grave).

REVERSED

Loneliness, deprivation, the feeling that life has passed one by, of being in a rut, fenced-in, entombed by an unhappy lifestyle (marriage, job, etc.).

Judgement

The World

KEY 21

DESCRIPTION

A naked young woman holds a wand in each hand. She is encircled by a wreath of leaves. The four corners of this card depict the same four animals of Ezekiel as on Key 10: The Wheel of Fortune. In this instance, though, only the heads are shown. This is the last card of the Tarot . . . The Fool has reached the end of his journey.

SYMBOLISM

The wreath represents both Nature and the crown of the initiate on life's journey, given to those who have learned to master the four guardians (kingdoms, elements, etc.). Self-mastery. The wreath itself forms a magic circle around the woman, symbolizing self-protection. She has risen above both the threats and the temptations of the world.

MEANING

Cosmic knowledge, worldly awareness, universal insight, truth. The journey has ended, the circle completes itself, the facts of life are learned, the ability to be "in tune with the times," to adapt oneself to changes, new ideas, trends, mores. As the world turns, so do the adept, right along with it. "The world is his oyster." Completion, a job well done, success, material and spiritual manifestation, cosmic consciousness, mastering the world instead of letting it master him (or her), colloquially "rolling with the punches."

REVERSED

Fear of change, the "world stands still," stagnancy, one who never learns, refuses to budge, stubbornly sticking to sameness, resisting change, left behind while others forge ahead, reactionary rather than progressive.

The World

Five

The Minor Arcana

The fifty-six cards in the Minor Arcana correspond to the fifty-two cards in the regular deck. They are interpreted in the same way. The one difference is that there is an extra "Jack" (both a Knight and a Page) in each suit.

To simplify matters, Wands are Clubs, Cups are Hearts, Swords are Spades, and Pentacles are Diamonds.

The extra "Jack" helps give more dimension to the reading. It is an additional picture card to concentrate on.

The meanings given to each card here are to help you learn their symbolism, to identify with each card, to get you started. These are idea-starters, psychic instigators, but they are not stagnant pasteboards. A too literal, cut-and-dried reading lacks "soul," and is dull and possibly worthless. The whole point of these card meanings is to give you a foundation for their interpretation. They are a focal point of psychic concentration, a way of releasing the subconscious, a means toward an end, but they are not an end in themselves.

The difference between a good Tarot interpreter and a bad one is the same as that between a good painter and a mediocre one. The latter paints strictly according to the rules. The former utilizes all the rules but isn't limited to or restricted by them, and this is what you should do. Never hesitate to express whatever thoughts or images come into your mind. Between mind and matter (Tarot cards), between a literal reading of the cards and an intuitively enlightened one, you'll be amazed at the revelations this combination brings.

PENTACLES

Element: Earth; Direction: East; Regular Deck: Diamonds

Pentacles represent money, wealth, finances, paychecks, salaries, taxes, luxuries, jewelry, bank accounts, savings, stocks and bonds, mutual funds, security, inheritances, bonuses, raises, gratuities, promotions, gains, gambling commissions, social security, pensions, welfare checks, old-age assistance, personal possessions, things of value, *objets d'art*, safe deposit boxes, wills, real estate, property, "money to burn," and financial security.

In Medieval times, Pentacles symbolized the Merchant or Tradesman. Today they represent material success, worldly goods, the professional or businessman (or woman), freedom from financial worry, affluence, and the belief that "diamonds are a girl's best friend." Whether called pentacles, coins, or diamonds, the symbolism is the same. "From rags to riches" is still the great American dream. If most people had a choice between "freedom" and "security," they'd choose the latter. Yet wealth does not free one from the tyranny of life. True, "money doesn't buy happiness," but it certainly helps to make one's life comfortable. And the unhappy poor person will gladly change places with the unhappy rich person!

Since money is an inanimate object, one's attitude toward it reveals much about one's character. A person really can't despise money, only the virtues or vices involved in its acquisition. People who say they "hate money" are those who haven't earned it or who got it dishonorably. Those who "worship" money reveal psychological insecurities. To them, money means protection, safety, a defense against hurt. To be fully enjoyed, money must be regarded as a reward for virtue, compensation for a job well done, just compensation for labor expended.

Ace of Pentacles

DESCRIPTION

A hand protrudes from a cloud holding a golden circle with the pentagram. Below this is a garden of flowers.

MEANING

Ace high, top position, A-1 condition, an important letter or document, a ring (friendship or engagement), getting a degree such as Ph.D., M.A., B.A., D.D., a profitable tip or information, a letter of acceptance, appointment, or confirmation. A visa or passport. A contract, license, permit, letter of introduction to an important person. Ace of Diamonds.

RHYMED MESSAGE

> Ace of Pentacles a girl's best friend,
> A beau's best bet to insure a blend!

COMBINATIONS

Near the Ten of Cups means a marriage. Near the Ace of Swords may mean an important letter held, or deception about a ring (the promise of one, or perhaps a married man claiming to be otherwise!). Near The Lovers, an engagement. Near The High Priestess, the beginning of occult knowledge. Near The Tower, a broken engagement. Near The Sun or The Star, one's ambitions realized—attaining a high position. Near The Hanged Man and Swords, a seemingly good offer causing indecisiveness. (Example: A woman given an engagement ring: she likes the man but is not sure if she wants to marry him. Or, the offer or appointment to a good position that may have more responsibilities than one wants!) Near the Death card, implies being left something in a will.

Ace of Pentacles

Two of Pentacles

DESCRIPTION

A young man dressed like a jester is dancing. In his hands are two pentagrams enjoined by a rope that forms the number eight. Behind him are two ships riding the high waves.

MEANING

A small check, letter containing good news (a bank statement, refund, dividend, etc.). A jewelry set (earrings, cuff links, matching necklace and bracelet, a pair of candlesticks). Making a small profit. A "lucky" piece (medal, coin, perhaps a silver dollar). A button with an insignia (usually indicating membership in some organization).

RHYMED MESSAGE

> Two of Pentacles good news or small check,
> A small sum of money you will collect.

COMBINATIONS

Near the Five or Six of Swords means the misplacement or loss of a small check, bank statement, or sum of money (jewelry too). When combined with The Devil, indicates someone who steals (pilfers) small sums of money. Near The Star, indicates the achievement of small goals. Near The Lovers, a small gift from a loved one. Near The Fool, suggests one who is "penny wise and pound foolish," especially if other Sword cards are nearby. Near The Chariot or Four of Wands, a small decoration or ornament for the car, some minor new addition.

Two of Pentacles

Three of Pentacles

DESCRIPTION

A young man is working in a monastery or church, watched
by two others. He seems to be a sculptor. The top part of
the card has three Pentacles in a trinity.

MEANING

This card usually refers to one's work, good or bad, determined by surrounding cards. Craftsmanship, skill, profes-
sionalism, ability to think in abstract principles, creative
ideas in commerce, business, and industry (the "brain
trust," "think tanks," or "idea banks" maintained by many
large corporations).

RHYMED MESSAGE

> Three of Pentacles is the work you do,
> A chance to rise is your lot too.

COMBINATIONS

Falling near The High Priestess, a highly mystical interpretation, the beginning of occult insight, an initiate into the
Older Mysteries. Near The Devil (especially if reversed),
an interest in Satanism or the dark arts. Followed by other
Pentacles, indicates an increase in salary, promotion, ad-
vancement. With the Five or Six of Swords and Eight of
Swords, the loss of a job. Near the Wheel of Fortune, a
job or position that has a future. Near The Lovers, possibility of "romance on the job" or meeting someone through
work that leads to such.

Three of Pentacles

Four of Pentacles

DESCRIPTION

A man is sitting down with two pentacles at his feet, one above his head, and the other clasped and encircled by his arms. A city is seen in the distance.

MEANING

This is a highly constructive card, one indicating a firm foundation, business stability, "having both feet on the ground." Specifically sound business judgement, a desk, safety deposit box, cashier's window, a place where valuables are kept, bankbook or savings account, "a blueprint for success." A gift. Hope chest.

RHYMED MESSAGE

> Four of Pentacles is a success plan
> Formed by the future-oriented man.

COMBINATIONS

With three other fours, indicates a seminar conference, convention, "congregation of the clan." Near high Sword cards, indicates one who hasn't planned well, a faulty premise. With other pentacles, means expansion and material success. Near the Wheel of Fortune with no sword cards, means success. Near The Sun or The Star, the realization of one's practical aspirations. Near The High Priestess or The Magician, indicates that one uses occult knowledge in a practical way. Also means an altar (in one's home). Near The Tower, means bankruptcy. Near The Fool, a warning to double-check your plans, so as not to build on quicksand.

Four of Pentacles

Five of Pentacles

DESCRIPTION

Two people, a man who is lame and walking on crutches, and a destitute woman, pass by a lighted window decorated with five pentacles. They are walking in a snowstorm.

MEANING

In a reading, this card's symbolism of destitution applies only if surrounded by Swords. This is the midway point in one's life, a time when one gets tired of the struggle, yet may be on the verge of success. Specifically refers to legal papers, contracts, documents, briefs, summonses, affidavits, notarized statements, licenses, confidential reports made by the CIA, FBI, police. Clearing up of important legal matters.

RHYMED MESSAGE

Five of Pentacles is a matter legal
You have to be sharp-eyed like the eagle!

COMBINATIONS

If this falls near any two Knights, it means a court case. With the Five or Six of Swords and any other high Sword card, it means losing a legal case. With The Devil and Swords, a warning to be careful of participating in any kind of illicit, illegal, or get-rich quick scheme. Near the Ten of Pentacles and the Seven of Pentacles, an inheritance or possibly winning a lottery. Followed by the Wheel of Fortune, The Sun, or The Star, success is just around the corner. Near The Tower, it means financial disaster.

Five of Pentacles

Six of Pentacles

DESCRIPTION

A businessman weighs money on the scales held in his left hand. With his right hand he is distributing coins to two kneeling beggars.

MEANING

Having more than enough to meet one's needs, thus in a position to donate to charity. Specifically, a raise, promotion, or bonus. A profit-sharing opportunity. The threat of the Five of Pentacles has been met and overcome: he is no longer preoccupied with worrying about money. A raise in one's standard of living.

RHYMED MESSAGE

> Six of Pentacles is the looked-for raise,
> Paycheck and promotion, the best praise!

COMBINATIONS

With The World, means that things all-around are changing for the better, things are starting to happen. Near The Devil and other Pentacles, means temptation to self-indulgence. Near The Moon, indicates "moonlighting," holding down a second or part-time job, possibly at night. Near The Hanged Man and the Eight of Swords, a warning to slow down, take it easy, learn to relax, get a better perspective on things: it can't be all work and no play. Near The Tower, this warns of false security: put something aside for a rainy day. With another six it means things coming to a conclusion, completion, "a job well done." With the Ten of Pentacles, represents savings, a growing bank account, the ability to save regularly.

Six of Pentacles

Seven of Pentacles

DESCRIPTION

A young man leans on a staff or wand (possibly a hoe) and looks down on a bush bearing seven pentacles. A "money tree"?

MEANING

This is the fate, luck, or gamble card. The true meaning of "luck" is depicted in this card: work, effort, and application. A change for the better in one's luck or finances. Gambling of any kind, bingo, lottery, playing the numbers, taking a chance, and speculation in the stock market. Getting or winning money without work, a prize, lottery, win.

RHYMED MESSAGE

> Seven of Pentacles is a change in your luck,
> The "winning way" is to change it to PLUCK!

COMBINATIONS

With the Wheel of Fortune and other pentacles it means being "lucky with money," a wise investment, possibility of "making a killing" in the stock market. Surrounded by spades, danger of losing money through gambling or speculation. Near The Tower, indicates someone who has gambled his life away: security, family, home. Destruction through unwise investments. Near the Judgement card, a warning to be sensible, play small, or only that which you can afford to lose. With The Devil and Swords, it indicates the type of self-delusion that thinks "With my winnings I'll be able to pay off all my debts," and loses! Near The Lovers and other Cup cards, "Lucky in love."

Seven of Pentacles

Eight of Pentacles

DESCRIPTION

A craftsman at work, chisel in one hand, hammer in the other, seated on a bench. He is working on one pentacle, while seven others are on display.

MEANING

Conscientiousness, initiative, application, dedication to one's work resulting in extra money, more income, being "ahead in the game," having financial resources, putting something (money) aside, good work habits and systematic savings, persistence and stick-to-it-iveness that eventually pays off.

RHYMED MESSAGE

> The Eight of Pentacles means extra money
> It's the "busy bee" that gets the "honey"!

COMBINATIONS

Eight, Nine, and Ten of Pentacles together mean riches, luxuries, a person of wealth, financial affluence, etc. With the Eight of Swords, a need to "balance the budget." With The Devil, a temptation to spend more than one should, With Death, the Five of Pentacles, and two Knights, means getting money via a will or inheritance. With The Magician, someone who has the "golden touch," everything he touches turns to gold. Near The Hanged Man, a warning not to let money go to your head and don't lose your sense of values. Don't think that money is a substitute for character, culture, or achievement. Near The Tower, indicates your security is in danger, a threat of financial loss.

Eight of Pentacles

Nine of Pentacles

DESCRIPTION

A stately woman is standing in a garden with a bird perched on her hand. She is surrounded by grapevines and the nine pentacles.

MEANING

This suggests living in splendor, comfort, enjoyment of all that money can buy. Specifically, a big check, high finance, an executive salary. Can also be read as any check from the state such as social security, welfare, unemployment, civil service, tax refund, disability, compensation. Someone employed by the government or state.

RHYMED MESSAGE

> Nine of Pentacles is a big check you can expect.
> Tax refund, stock dividend, or new monied project!

COMBINATIONS

With the Ace of Swords and the Five of Pentacles (and other Swords), trouble with taxes. With the Nine of Cups, it means both personal and professional fulfillment. Next to two or three tens, money spent on travel. If The Sun is nearby, it indicates going to a sunny climate (Florida, California, Bahamas, etc.). Near The Chariot, suggests buying a new car (if no high Sword cards are nearby). Near the Wheel of Fortune, it means one's financial good luck continues and grows and steady checks result from same (dividends, royalties, etc.). Near the Ace of Swords and the Five or Six of Swords, indicates bad checks, insufficient funds, being overdrawn on one's bank account.

Nine of Pentacles

Ten of Pentacles

DESCRIPTION

An older man, a patriarch, sits in a garden surrounded by
his family and two dogs. Leading to an elegant house, an
archway is emblazoned with his coat of arms.

MEANING

This suggests a man of wealth, social position, prestige,
one who has "made a name for himself." Specifically,
wealth, the career card, success, a bank, the idea of "money
to burn," freedom from financial fear, professional attainment and recognition, high finance or "big money," security for life.

RHYMED MESSAGE

> Ten of Pentacles is success and achievement
> You need never fear financial bereavement!

COMBINATIONS

With the Ten of Cups, it means "Health, Wealth, and Happiness." Surrounded by Sword cards, one's career, finances, or security is in danger. Near The Tower, a career
that is destroyed, a life ruined, especially with other high
Sword cards. Near The Devil and Sword cards, secret
enemies. With The Fool, Sword cards, and no Cups nearby,
one who has concentrated so much on material wealth and
possessions that he's alienated family and friends and lives
in lonely splendor. Near The High Priestess and no Sword
cards, one who uses his wealth to pioneer new fields, en-
dows research into parapsychology, ESP, a highly developed individual. Four tens indicates world travel.

Ten of Pentacles

Page of Pentacles

DESCRIPTION

A young figure seems oblivious to his surroundings while staring fixedly at a pentacle held in his hands.

SYMBOLISM

Concentration, undivided attention.

COLORING

Very fair, blond to light brown hair, blue, gray, or green eyes.

DEPICTION

A young person, may be a boy or girl: a teenager, the "fair haired boy."

COMMENTS

Must be read in relation to all the other cards. Often, the Pages are read as the "thoughts" of the King (of the same suit). Could be a blond child or young person, the sons of the Queen of Pentacles (or possibly any other Queen, since the child may take after a light father rather than a darker mother). A good student, scholarly, attentive, one who prefers solitude and books rather than sports.

Page of Pentacles

Knight of Pentacles

DESCRIPTION

A knight rides a dark horse, seemingly balancing the pentacle in his right hand, but not looking directly at it.

SYMBOLISM

Joining the ranks of the gainfully employed, carefully weighing advantages, methodical.

COLORING

Very fair, blond to light brown hair, blue, gray, or green eyes.

DEPICTION

A young man of the above coloring, usually one just starting on a career or new job.

COMMENTS

A young man who means business, out to conquer the world, make a name for himself, ambitious, materialistic, careful, going slow at first since he lacks the confidence of experience, but nevertheless *going*. May be the son, brother, or beau of woman being read. The card itself suggests the ambitious young man who isn't going to take any chances, who plans his work and works his plan.

Knight of Pentacles

Queen of Pentacles

DESCRIPTION

Sitting on her throne, a queen gazes at a pentacle she is holding on her lap. The throne is covered with symbolic figures: Cupid, ripe fruit, and goat heads. Above her hang roses, while on her right is a rabbit.

SYMBOLISM

Peace and plenty, material comfort, fruitfulness, practical creativeness.

COLORING

Very fair, usually blond (or hair dyed that color), with blue, gray, or green eyes.

DEPICTION

A woman of above coloring.

COMMENTS

The suggestion that "diamonds are a girl's best friend." The Queen of Pentacles can be anything from a natural blond to one who bleaches her hair! Can be read as an older, white-haired woman. Generally, this card depicts a showgirl type: flashy, bedecked in jewelry, exhibitionist, beauty-parlor blond. Depending upon surrounding cards, may be a gold-digger type, a female executive, or a woman more interested in luxury than in love.

Queen of Pentacles

King of Pentacles

DESCRIPTION

A king in rich robes sits on his throne, holding the pentacle in his left hand and a globe-headed wand in his right. His robe is richly decorated with the symbols of fruitfulness. The throne is decorated with bulls' heads. A castle is seen in the background.

SYMBOLISM

A wealthy man, business tycoon, industrialist, self-made man, "King of all he surveys."

COLORING

Very fair, blond, gray, or light brown hair (touches of gray), with blue, gray, or green eyes.

DEPICTION

An older man of above coloring.

COMMENTS

The above symbolism may or may not apply, depending on person getting the reading. May be the husband, father, or boyfriend of woman being read. The card itself represents a man who has "made it," and is secure, successful, and possibly titled. Certainly a "man of means." An authority figure, more a "father image" than a "father" (symbolically speaking . . . he could have children, too).

King of Pentacles

SWORDS

Element: Air; Direction: North; Regular Deck: Spades

Swords represent aggressive action, power, force, militancy, fighting, quarrels, hatred, violence, war, sickness, fear, worry, aggravations, anxiety, reverses, losses, tragedies, accidents, disharmony, broken friendships, marriages, homes, divorce, frustration, deception, wrongdoing, evil, theft, hostility, ill will, hurt feelings, insults, neuroses, psychoses, bitterness, obstacles, burdens, troubles, friction, resentments, impositions, tensions, pressures, jealousy, delays, and enemies.

In medieval times, Swords symbolized the nobility. They ruled by force, waged war, and gained wealth and lands by conquest. The "Divine Right of Kings" was enforced by the sword. Those who disobeyed them were "put to the sword." In its worst form, the sword is symbolical of power-lust, brutality, and despotism. At best, it represents courage, the fighter for truth, the defender of man's rights. And though swords indicate trouble or turmoil, it's also true that "you can't clean house without stirring up some of the dust." Sometimes you have to get worse before you can get better (undergoing an operation, having a "showdown" with a bully, standing up for your rights).

Swords symbolize the mysterious, forbidden, unknown, darker aspects of life. When applied psychologically, they indicate uncertainty, self-doubt, someone who hasn't "found himself." They can refer to both the underground and the underworld, the so-called "Black Arts," and anti-establishment political activities. This also includes those whose work is secretive and "undercover" such as the FBI, CIA, detectives, police, spies, drug pushers, revolutionaries, sado-masochistic clubs, and those who live outside the law.

Ace of Swords

DESCRIPTION

A hand holding an upright sword juts from a cloud. The Sword is topped by a crown, from which hangs a laurel and an olive branch. There are six yods descending, symbolizing the spirit.

MEANING

Analogous to the Ace of Spades in the regular deck. Often called the death card. Really a worried mind, doubt, delay, setback, bad news, the need to fight for one's rights, trouble, anxiety, expecting the worst. Interference in one's plans, being blocked, fearful anticipation. When this card touches the person being read, indicates one who is "sick with worry," depressed, sad.

RHYMED MESSAGE

> Ace of Swords means delay and worry,
> Better get things done in a hurry!

COMBINATIONS

When this falls near The Devil it means "your past catching up with you." Whether the delay or worry is justified, or, if so, permanent, is determined by surrounding cards. Near The Moon, means underhanded activity. Near The Magician, one who uses deception and trickery. With The Tower and Death cards, represents death of someone and possible disaster. Near The Star, indicates wrong aspirations, false hopes. Near The Hanged Man, the idea that "give him enough rope and he'll hang himself." Near The Fool, indicates that one is being deceived as to the true intentions of another. Near The World, the attitude that "The world's wrong and I'm right."

Ace of Swords

Two of Swords

DESCRIPTION

A blindfolded figure is seated holding two swords. Her arms are crossed and balanced on her shoulders. Her back is to the sea. A crescent moon is in the sky.

MEANING

The idea suggested here is to "Hold your fire." A temporary truce, but the problem remains. Holding a grudge, hostility, resentment, an insult, a letter containing bad news, tears, ambivalence (two co-existing opposite emotions, like resentment and respect, love and hate). A sense of alienation, loneliness, angry self-protection, defensiveness, being on guard, someone with a "chip on his shoulder."

RHYMED MESSAGE

> Two of Swords is bad news
> Sadly you've got the blues!

COMBINATIONS

With the Ace of Swords indicates harsh words, vituperation, verbal fireworks. Near The Tower, destructive words that can't be taken back. Near The Devil, represents backbiting, vicious gossip, undermining one's character. Near The Fool, the results of listening to gossip making one angry without investigation. Falling near The Lovers, a warning that someone is trying to cause trouble between friends or a couple. Near The Sun, indicates that things are basically good, this is only a minor cloud. Near Death, may mean a sense of guilt over the loss of a loved one or family member.

Two of Swords

Three of Swords

DESCRIPTION

Three swords penetrate a heart. In the background there are clouds and rain. The card color is grey.

MEANING

Heartbroken, a feeling of being stabbed in the back, betrayed, third party interference, sorrow, melancholy, grief, disappointment. "Two's company, three's a crowd," thus an unwanted third person who imposes himself or tries to cause trouble, a miscarriage or abortion, constant bickering, fault finding, undermining criticism. Spite, a desire for revenge, the desire to get even after being emotionally exploited.

RHYMED MESSAGE

> Three of Swords means aggravations,
> Busybodies and broken relations.

COMBINATIONS

This with The Tower means a personal tragedy in one's life (like being "left at the altar" or one's fiancée being killed, etc.). With The Devil and The Magician, the practice of malevolent magic, especially if surrounded by other Sword cards. This may take the form of sending poison pen letters or hate mail. Near The Star, indicates having one's hopes dashed to the ground. Followed by The Sun, symbolizes that despite one's present heartbreak, he or she will be happy again: "Better days are coming." Near The Chariot, may indicate a car accident. Near The Lovers, means a breakup or divorce, especially if the Five or Six of Swords is near.

Three of Swords

Four of Swords

DESCRIPTION

A knight lies on his tomb. The top left of this card depicts a stained glass window. Three swords stand upright above him while the other one lies horizontally next to his tomb.

MEANING

A tomb, coffin, sick bed, funeral parlor. A feeling of being "sick of it all." Can be a sick room, hospital bed, infirmary. Does not represent death by itself though it could suggest going to a wake. Deep depression bringing on illness or vice-versa, the feeling that one has struggled in vain. Retreating into illness, depression, the need to "get away from it all."

RHYMED MESSAGE

> Four of Swords is your sick bed.
> Consoling thought: you're not dead!

COMBINATIONS

Near the Five or Six of Swords, means an operation. Near The Star, indicates that one's goals have a faulty foundation. With either The Chariot or the Four of Wands, trouble with one's car. Near the Wheel of Fortune, depression over one's sense of "bad luck." Building up false hopes of winning a lottery—this confirmed when the Seven of Pentacles is nearby with other Swords. Near The Devil and the Four of Cups, a fear of repercussions because of indiscretions or promiscuity. Near The Magician, indicates a false prophet, a phony healer, a spiritual fraud. Near Justice, represents getting sick through overindulgence or repercussions from refusing to recognize the possible consequences of one's behavior.

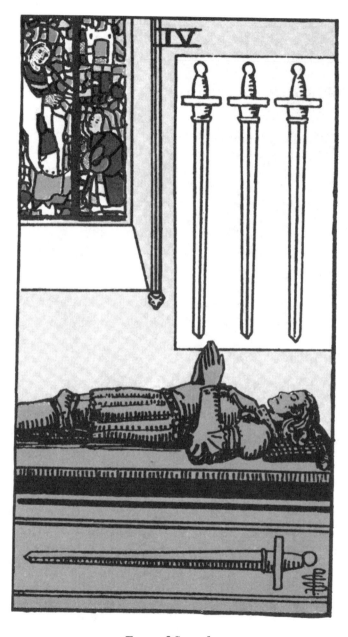

Four of Swords

Five of Swords

DESCRIPTION

A young man carrying two swords on his shoulder and another in his right hand looks with amusement or scorn at two dejected figures in back of him whose swords are on the ground. The sky is filled with storm clouds.

MEANING

The idea suggested here is one who gloats over his defeat of others, or who enjoys their misery. One who tries to rule by force, who "lives by the sword," insensitive and indifferent, a petty tyrant. May be an operation, a breakup, a split, severing of ties, breaking of bonds, losing something, a child running away, a theft, loss, being burglarized.

RHYMED MESSAGE

> Five of Swords is a separation
> Sometimes means an operation.

COMBINATIONS

Near the Four, Eight, or Nine of Spades, indicates a major operation. Near the Nine of Cups, it can be interpreted as "getting a break." Near any two fives, a warning: "Be careful of hurting your hands or legs." Near the Wheel of Fortune and other Swords, it indicates loss of an opportunity. Near The World with no prominent Swords nearby, just the feeling of "wanting to get away from it all" at times, taking a break. Near The Lovers, means a temporary break-up, permanent only if all the other cards are Swords. When this card falls near Pentacles, a warning as to loss or theft of valuables, money, or jewelry.

Five of Swords

Six of Swords

DESCRIPTION

A man with his back turned is ferrying a woman and a child in his boat to the opposite shore. There are six swords standing upright in front of him and his passengers.

MEANING

This card and the Five of Swords are somewhat inter-changeable. A break, cutting away (or out), in modern slang "splitting," taking leave, going away, parting, separa-tion, breaking of bonds, severing of ties, leaving behind. May mean a "parting of the ways," broken friendships, divorce. However, there are times when this is necessary: breaking away from bad relationships, "cutting out" of an unpleasant situation or frustrating job.

RHYMED MESSAGE

Six of Swords implies divorce
When there is no other recourse!

COMBINATIONS

With any two eights or tens, this card means that the parting or separation involves taking a trip. If followed by The Star or The Sun and other favorable cards, the reading is "It's the best thing you could have done." With Judgement card and other Swords it says, "Think twice before you act." Near The Fool, indicates that you may be acting im-pulsively, without forethought, the move isn't a wise one. Near The Magician, implies that the threat to leave or "quit" or whatever is a ploy, a pretense, rather than an actual desire. Near The Devil, indicates one who is trying to break a bad habit.

Six of Swords

Seven of Swords

DESCRIPTION

A man seems to be running away while carrying five swords. Two are left behind. In the background there is what looks like a military camp.

MEANING

A setback, a change for the worse, bad luck, reversal in plans, being hit with everything at once, trying to escape, evade, avoid, or desert such trouble, "on the lam" or "making a getaway," the feeling that "I had better get the hell out of here while I can." This card also has meanings that aren't negative: the water or drinking card from which is derived such meanings as sinks, bathroom, water pipes, refrigerator, etc. Also "having a drink" (of alcohol) from which is derived a bar, tavern, or nightclub. The water symbolism may come from the seven seas.

RHYMED MESSAGE

> Seven of Swords from feast to famine,
> "Drowning one's sorrows" leads to chagrin!

COMBINATIONS

Near the Wheel of Fortune and other Swords: "Everything has come to a standstill." With two or three other sevens, this means a complete change in every area of one's life. Near the Ace of Swords it means "getting drunk" or an alcoholic. Near The Fool, the suggestion that one is his own worst enemy: a changeable, inconsistent person, unable to make decisions and stick by them. Falling near Justice, means "Getting what he deserves." Near The Moon, implies erratic behavior, what people mean when they say "There must be a full moon out tonight." Near The Chariot and Swords, a warning of trouble with a car— you have to have it fixed or get a new one.

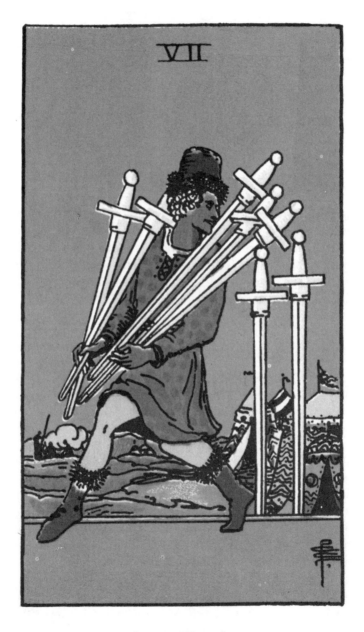

Seven of Swords

Eight of Swords

DESCRIPTION

A woman is bound and blindfolded, head bent. She is surrounded by upright swords. In the distance there is a castle.

MEANING

Disappointment, confusion, hurt, inability to see or think clearly, not knowing where to turn or what to do, overwhelmed with troubles or sickness. Health bears watching, illness as an escape from anxiety, frustration, disillusionment, disharmony, disruption. Always a warning to consult a doctor if surrounded by other swords. Being emotionally drained of energy, exhaustion.

RHYMED MESSAGE

> Eight of Swords is a big disappointment,
> "Health is Wealth" needs no further comment!

COMBINATIONS

Surrounded by high Sword cards, danger of a serious health condition, operation, with the Ace of Swords indicates death (especially if Death is near). If this card is surrounded by Pentacles and Cups, merely indicates anxiety, worry, "You're making a mountain out of a molehill." Near The Devil, anxiety as a mask for feelings of guilt. Near The Hanged Man, indicates being "shaken up" in some way. Near The Magician and small Sword cards, this means the feeling of having been trifled with or cheated. Near The Hierophant and other Swords: one who has turned his back on religion, especially the one in which he was brought up. Near the Lovers, a disappointing love affair.

Eight of Swords

Nine of Swords

DESCRIPTION

A woman sits on her bed, head held in her hands. Above her hang nine swords horizontally.

MEANING

Deepest despair, chronic illness, hopelessness, inconsolable grief, impending tragedy, adversity, a major operation, incurable illness (like terminal cancer), destitution, stark poverty, a sense of total abandonment, the feeling "I've got nothing to live for," utter futility, "life is just a vale of tears."

RHYMED MESSAGE

> Nine of Swords is a warning of danger
> Death is never a "Welcome Stranger."

COMBINATIONS

One must be very careful in reading any of the high Sword cards. When this falls with the Eight and Ace of Swords it reads Death. Otherwise a tragedy or very serious operation. When Cups or Pentacles or The Sun come after it, the meaning is simply, "You will pull through." Near The Chariot or the Four of Wands, danger of a car accident. Near the Ten of Swords, may indicate an accident on water or a drowning. (This should be read in a past tense, e.g., "Do you know anyone in the past who died of drowning?") Near the Seven of Spades, could indicate water pipes breaking, a flooding, etc. Near Justice, the reading may mean someone who has wronged others and is getting his "just desserts." Near Judgement, suggests not accepting something as final—one doctor's opinion, for example.

Nine of Swords

Ten of Swords

DESCRIPTION

A man lies prostrate on the ground with ten swords stuck into him. In the top part of the card is a blackened sky.

MEANING

Not in itself a death card, but the next thing to it. "I wish I were dead." Utter disaster, misfortune, loss of everything dear, complete collapse of one's plans, goals, or fortunes. "Everything looks black." Also means a large body of water (sea, ocean, lake). The underworld, underground, "those who dwell in darkness.

RHYMED MESSAGE

> Ten of Swords has many meanings,
> Shadowy, underworld leanings!

COMBINATIONS

With another ten, a trip on water. Three tens means an ocean voyage (cruise or flying over the ocean). With high Sword cards, represents the worst. With The High Priestess and no high Sword cards, one who is looking into the Mystery Religions, occult knowledge, intuition, subconscious awareness. Near The Devil, one attracted to the "dark arts" or involved in antisocial behavior. Near The Hanged Man, represents one who has gotten himself so deeply involved in wrong activities that he can't find his way out. Near The Lovers and other Sword cards, cynicism about love or ever having it.

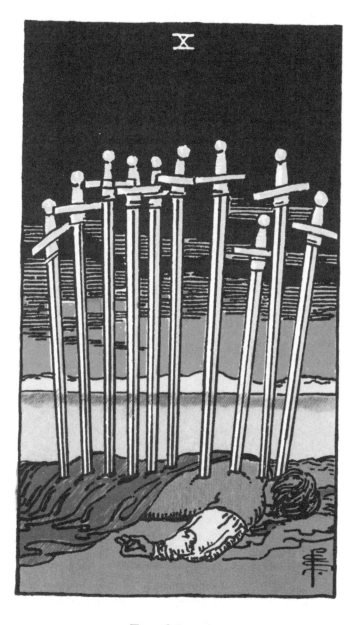

Ten of Swords

Page of Swords

DESCRIPTION

A young figure (man or maiden, not clear) holds a sword tightly in his hands while walking over rocky ground. Clouds surround him and he looks as if he's expecting someone to attack him.

SYMBOLISM

Being on guard, apprehensive, defensive, and self-protective.

COLORING

A very dark young person, brown to black hair, brown or black eyes.

DEPICTION

Person of above coloring.

COMMENTS

Again, the sexual ambiguity of this card suggests (whether intended or not) a young child, teenager, and possibly the young male adolescent who has to prove his masculinity by fighting, who uses aggressiveness as a defense against self-doubt, the "street-corner macho" type who brags to his friends about his imaginary sexual conquests. Can be either male or female teenager who has a "chip on the shoulder."

Page of Swords

Knight of Swords

DESCRIPTION

A young knight is galloping at full speed on his white horse, holding an upraised sword in his right hand, hell-bent on charging into the fray, attacking enemies.

SYMBOLISM

An aggressive young man, brave, combative, full of bravado, a defender of what he believes.

COLORING

Very dark young man, brown to black hair, brown or black eyes.

DEPICTION

A person of above coloring.

COMMENTS

Symbolically, this card can be either good or bad, depending upon surrounding cards. If near other Swords, it depicts an impulsive, headstrong, reckless young man, self-destructive, quick to take offense. If near Cups and Pentacles, a young man who has the "courage of his convictions," who is not afraid to take a stand, to defend those he loves. to "fight for the right." Archetype of romantic chivalry. A Sir Galahad type . . . or an ass.

Knight of Swords

Queen of Swords

DESCRIPTION

Looking over a cloudy horizon, a queen sits regally on her throne, stately, severe, with an upraised sword in her right hand, the left hand extended upward.

SYMBOLISM

Widowhood, divorced woman, sense of loneliness and deprivation, the need to struggle.

COLORING

Very dark woman with brown or black hair, brown or black eyes.

DEPICTION

A woman of above coloring.

COMMENTS

Often read for a widow (regardless of coloring). One who has to "go it alone." The woman who has to raise fatherless children (whether through death, divorce, or sudden departure). All of the court cards in the sword suit have many clouds, storm warnings, indicating trouble or troubled persons, friction, a struggle to maintain one's position, a sense of "nothing comes easy" and "I have to fight for everything that I get."

Queen of Swords

King of Swords

DESCRIPTION

Sitting erect on his throne, a king holds an unsheathed, upraised sword in his right hand. There are clouds and trees in the background.

SYMBOLISM

Power, authority, judgement, "a life and death matter," Establishment Justice.

COLORING

Very dark, with brown to black hair, brown or black eyes.

DEPICTION

A man of above coloring.

COMMENTS

Can represent police, judges, government officials, military men, undercover cops, agents provocateurs, spies, etc. Simply a very dark-complexioned man. In some readings, a very stern father who inflicted both verbal and physical abuse on his children (often found in the background of prostitutes). When surrounded by swords, a very mean man, a bully and tyrant, one who abuses his position of power; what has been termed a "hanging judge."

King of Swords

CUPS

Element: Water; Direction: West; Regular Deck: Hearts

Cups represent love and marriage (with or without a carriage!). Symbol of the womb, femininity, pleasure, emotions, friendships, liaisons, "affairs of the heart," romance, goodwill, benevolence, kindness, sincerity, affection, loved ones, family, home, happiness, joy, trust, honesty, fair play, good relationships, communication, sexual attraction, "having a good time," peace of mind, robust health, fertility, emotional security, "joie de vivre," tenderness, flirtation, harmony, "the horn of plenty," festivities, "in his cups," and "my cup runneth over."

In medieval times, cups symbolized the clergy (chalice). The "loving cup" still holds true today, whether used sacramentally or in drinking a toast. An emotionally mature, sexually gratified person is usually a happy person who radiates peace and contentment and is tolerant of the foibles of others. He has none of the jealousy and hostility of those who are frustrated, whose thwarted love life manifests itself in violence directed toward others.

Cups symbolize the life-force, the creative impulse: whether giving birth to a baby, a book, an idea, or an invention, the procreative instinct used constructively. Sex, whether expressed, suppressed, or repressed, sought out or sublimated, used or abused, whether a substitute for self-esteem or an expression of it, will be determined by what cards surround cups in the layout. In themselves, cups are always positive.

Ace of Cups

DESCRIPTION

A hand is protruding out of a cloud holding a cup from which there are four streams pouring into the one below. A white dove holds a wafer in his beak with the sign of the cross.

MEANING

This is primarily the home card, a house, environment, surroundings. Wherever one resides, hotel, motel, or apartment. Place of origin "from whence thy came thou shall return." A "first love." Same as the Ace of Hearts in the regular deck. All cups refer to love, the emotions, positive feelings. A new start.

RHYMED MESSAGE

> Ace of Cups is Hearth and Home
> A place from which you'll never roam!

COMBINATIONS

Surrounded by Swords, this indicates trouble, turmoil, aggravations in the home, the seriousness determined by whether Swords are high or low cards. Falling next to The Tower, danger of a fire, earthquake, or some other calamity. Near The Hermit, it means either that one lives alone or, though amongst others, has a feeling of alienation. Falling near The Devil, it indicates that one is tempted to use his home for nefarious, illicit, or illegal activities. If this falls near The Magician or The High Priestess, may indicate someone engaged in occult work in his home (of whatever kind, including giving readings). If this card falls near The Fool, it's a warning that precautions should be taken to protect oneself: a new lock, window gates, faulty wiring, etc.

Ace of Cups

Two of Cups

DESCRIPTION

A young man and woman seem to be drinking a toast, pledging themselves to each other. Above the cups is a caduceus and above that a winged lion's head.

MEANING

Simply a pair, two of a kind, good news, love letter and/or letter from a loved one, a word of praise, a bouquet of flowers, beginning of a new romance, flirtation, "making goo-goo eyes," puppy love, a symbol of how long it will be before your wish comes true, friendship, sympathy, affection, a kind word, an expression of thoughtfulness.

RHYMED MESSAGE

> Two of Cups is love and good news
> Happy hint of future "I do's!"

COMBINATIONS

With The Fool, indicates a foolish flirtation or infatuation. Near The Devil, temptation to indiscretion. Near The Tower, this means "It's strictly bad news." Falling near The Chariot, indicates riding with a loved one in some sort of vehicle, not excluding carnival rides and the "love tunnel." Surrounded by The Sun and other Cups or Pentacles, the beginning of a long-lasting relationship. Same is true if near The Lovers, which only serves to emphasize its meaning. If near The Hanged Man, it indicates "having your head turned around." Heart rather than head rules, need to get things in true perspective.

Two of Cups

Three of Cups

DESCRIPTION

Three young women raise their cups in joy, celebration, a pledge of friendship. They seem to be in a garden of fruit and vegetables.

MEANING

This suggests a bridal shower. Similar to the Three of Hearts in the regular deck. Often read as a child (the result of one and one). A pregnancy. The start of spiritual, mystic, or occult interests (the triangle, trinity, pyramid, etc.). A friendly third party. This is a pleasant, happy, fulfilling card, one denoting joy, anticipation (of marriage?), gaiety.

RHYMED MESSAGE

> Three of Cups is always an occasion
> Result of parental collaboration!

COMBINATIONS

If surrounded by Swords, may indicate a love triangle. With the Four of Cups and The Devil, possibility of a *ménage à trois*. Falling near The Tower, it means that someone is out to break up your friendship or romance with another. Near Death, may mean a miscarriage or abortion, death of a child. Should the Three of Cups fall near The High Priestess and all other cards near it are Cups or Pentacles, this foretells work in occult-mystic areas and a high degree of success with same. Falling near The Fool, a warning to "grow up and stop acting like a child." Or, put uncharitably, "Stop making an ass of yourself!"

Three of Cups

Four of Cups

DESCRIPTION

A young man, arms folded, knees crossed, sits on the grass and leans against a tree. A hand holding a cup is extended to him, while three other cups sit upright in front of him.

MEANING

This card implies that sometimes you can have too much of a good thing. The young man is not reaching out for the cup extended to him. Rather, he's contemplating the offer. This card is the love bed—four legs on a bed or couch plus pleasure! Can mean a party, bridal shower, stag party, entertaining at home, sexual attraction, having a good time.

RHYMED MESSAGE

>Four of Cups is an expression of love.
>If Swords are near it, frustration thereof!

COMBINATIONS

Falling near the Ace of Pentacles and the Ten of Cups means marriage. Near The Devil and two or three Swords, a warning of sexual excess, possible danger of venereal disease. Near The Fool and Swords, a warning that one is foolishly infatuated but that the love isn't reciprocated. Near The Tower and Swords, an infatuation or affair that can bring disaster (broken home, loss of respect, etc.). Near The World surrounded by Cups and Pentacles, the feeling that "love makes the world go 'round."

Four of Cups

Five of Cups

DESCRIPTION

A figure in a long black cloak has his back turned, head bowed, with two cups standing upright and three that have fallen. In the distance a small bridge leads to a castle.

MEANING

First impression is "two out of five." The sense of loss or regret is more a *feeling* rather than a fact. The three over-turned cups are neither broken nor lost. Only their contents are lost, and these can be replenished. Brings to mind the old saying about "Crying over spilt milk!" The midway point in one's personal life where one has to take stock, reevaluate things. Can mean "the hand of friendship" or "a helping hand" (five fingers). Sympathy, tenderness, holding hands; a tendency to brood over a minor emotional matter.

RHYMED MESSAGE

> Five of Cups is a helping hand
> Enabling you to understand.

COMBINATIONS

Falling with any other five, this represents two hands—yours (sometimes feet). Your goals, wishes, and life are in your own hands. Near The Sun, means good fortune. If Swords are near this, represents clouds, which will pass (figuratively speaking). Near The Tower, can mean self-destructive tendencies. Near The Devil, an admonition: "Play with fire and you'll get burned." Near Death, a warning that "You're digging your own grave." Falling near the Wheel of Fortune, suggests that it's up to you to make your own future, to turn the "wheel of fortune" yourself instead of waiting for it to happen.

Five of Cups

Six of Cups

DESCRIPTION

Two children, one holding a cup, stand in a garden in front of a cottage. Impression is one of "children at play."

MEANING

Happy times, emotional memories, nostalgia, a childlike sense of delight and wonder, trust, and creativity. Can mean a new friend, artistic or literary interests, good relationships, a sense of completion or fulfillment, a children's playground. An older meaning was a book from which is derived study, learning, knowledge.

RHYMED MESSAGE

Six of Cups is a friend in need,
Revealed to you by thought and deed.

COMBINATIONS

Falling near The Tower, indicates a childhood tragedy. Near The Hanged Man, means one who tends to regress to childish ways . . . immaturity. If near The High Priestess, it indicates an interest in the occult or religions of the past, especially those that worship a Goddess. If near The Magician, a person who has an interest in magical practices and the occult, ranging from "magic as a hobby" to the Cabala. Falling near The Devil with no Swords nearby, means a person who like to play practical jokes on others, impish ways, one who likes to put people on." Near The Emperor followed by Swords, indicates a lack of closeness to one's father. Near The Empress with Swords, a sense of alienation from one's mother.

Six of Cups

Seven of Cups

DESCRIPTION

A man is gazing at seven cups rising from the clouds, all of which contain jewels, wreaths, figures of a head, snake, castle, etc. A dreamlike card.

MEANING

This card suggests two sayings: "One who builds castles in the air" and "It never rains . . . it pours." Since all sevens imply change, this card indicates difficulty in making up one's mind in choosing which "cup" (goal, path, opportunity) is best to pursue. Generally means a change for the better, one that will bring about an unexpected but very much desired condition. "My cup runneth over." Winning out, conquering, victory.

RHYMED MESSAGE

> Seven of Cups is a change for the better,
> Take advantage by being a "go-getter."

COMBINATIONS

If surrounded by Swords or The Tower, this means a change that looks good on the surface but is fraught with danger. Near The Star, indicates the realization of one's goals through making a change. Near The Moon, this card warns to make sure that you are not overlooking certain factors (like the fine print in a contract!). Near Justice followed by Cups or Swords, could mean winning a court case, settlement, having a wrong righted. Near The Lovers, a change in one's love life, a new romance, or "things getting serious." Near The Hanged Man, suggests that reversing your position, "changing your ways," brings happy results.

Seven of Cups

Eight of Cups

DESCRIPTION

A man holding a staff is walking away from eight cups that are standing upright. He seems to be heading toward the mountains. A moon with an expressionless face is looking down on him.

MEANING

This suggests that one has had material success and is now looking for personal gratification or spiritual fulfillment. His walking away from the cups doesn't necessarily indicate abandonment, just a search for other things. It means double love, reciprocation, "the feeling's mutual." Symbolizes equality, value for value, as above so below, balance, emotional equilibrium. He has the material advantages and is now looking for something (more likely someone) to share them with.

RHYMED MESSAGE

> Eight of Cups is fair play and romance
> In "affairs of the heart" rules out chance!

COMBINATIONS

With The Lovers and Justice, a perfect combination. With the Eight of Swords, indicates being pulled in two different directions: the good and the bad, up and down (thus, in a minor way, one on a diet, losing weight). With the Wheel of Fortune, "lucky in love." With The World, indicates stability, security, "things running smoothly." Near The High Priestess, means achieving stability and tranquility in one's life by devotion to the Goddess (or in the private worship of one of the Old Religions). If near Death surrounded by Cups or Pentacles, symbolizes being reborn psychologically or spiritually (the rehabilitated alcoholic, criminal, or drug addict).

Eight of Cups

Nine of Cups

DESCRIPTION

A man with a happy expression on his face sits on a bench with his arms folded. Behind him, above his head, are nine cups in a row, forming a semi-circular arch.

MEANING

Happiness, contentment, fulfillment, abundance. This is the wish card and any time it ends a layout it means "You get your wish." Whether this attainment is easy or difficult will depend, of course, upon preceding and/or surrounding cards. This is the fulfillment of the search depicted in the Eight of Cups. One of the best cards in the Minor Arcana.

RHYMED MESSAGE

> Nine of Cups . . . Highest of all the cards
> "You get your wish" and "Happy Regards!"

COMBINATIONS

This card, falling near any of the following, emphasizes its value—a "sure to come true" reading: The Empress, The Magician, Justice, The Sun, The Star, The Lovers, The World, the Wheel of Fortune, and The High Priestess. If near Death or The Tower and surrounded by Swords, it indicates that one will *not* get his wish, will be very disappointed. Near The Devil, suggests that there is someone jealous of you and working surreptitiously to undermine your chances for happiness. Near The Fool, surrounded by basically good cards, indicates a few mistakes or errors in judgement, but nothing disastrous.

Nine of Cups

Ten of Cups

DESCRIPTION

The top part of this card shows two cups in a rainbow. Below this are a man and woman with their arms around each other, with two children, a boy and a girl, holding hands and dancing. Suggests a man and his wife and their two children.

MEANING

Marriage, a happy home, domestic bliss, a full life, that which makes all that preceded this worthwhile, peace of mind, emotional fulfillment, "a dream come true," gratification in love, "the pot at the end of the rainbow."

RHYMED MESSAGE

> Ten of Cups is happiness and peace of mind,
> "My cup runneth over." Life's so good and kind.

COMBINATIONS

This card falling next to the Nine of Cups reinforces the latter. When it is surrounded by Swords or The Tower, it means that one's happiness is only a temporary state or an illusion, that it won't last. Near The Magician, may indicate the use of love potions, charms, spells, amulets, or rituals to either get or sustain love (or subtler forms involving psychology, make-up, self-improvement, etc.). Near The Chariot and one or two other tens, indicates a change of states, traveling, a marriage that takes one to live in another country. Near Judgement and some Swords, a warning not to take a loved one, romance, or marriage for granted. Happiness can be spoiled by growing resentments.

Ten of Cups

Page of Cups

DESCRIPTION

Waite describes it as "a fair, pleasing, somewhat effeminate page." He is holding a cup in his right hand out of which protrudes a fish.

SYMBOLISM

Thought forms, images, ideas taking shape.

COLORING

Medium coloring, usually blue, gray, or green eyes, from sandy to medium brown hair.

DEPICTION

Young child, boy or girl, adolescent.

COMMENTS

You may read this card for a girl. There is another subtle connotation here: The stereotyped image of a homosexual as being "effeminate," or "girlish." The term generally used is "gay." Proceed with caution on this matter unless brought up by the subject. Can also mean a sensitive, retiring, shy young man, more interested in books and culture than in sports, without any implication of homosexuality whatsoever.

Page of Cups

Knight of Cups

DESCRIPTION

A young man is riding a gray horse. He holds a cup in his right hand. He wears a winged helmet. The horse is about to cross the stream. Mountains are in the distance.

SYMBOLISM

A young man going out to meet life, neither overly aggressive nor fearful, but with firm resolve.

COLORING

Medium coloring, usually blue, gray, or green eyes, from sandy to medium brown hair.

DEPICTION

A person of above coloring.

COMMENTS

Surrounded by other Knights and Pages, may indicate a college, fraternity, academy, military school, college, university. Generally a young man just "starting out," beginning a career, determined but aware that the future (the distant mountain peaks) holds many obstacles (uncertainty, the draft, examinations, getting that first job, etc.).

Knight of Cups

Queen of Cups

DESCRIPTION

A queen sits on her throne contemplating an ornately decorated cup. Cupids adorn the throne, which is surrounded
by water.

SYMBOLISM

Romance and reality enjoined, one's dreams backed up by
deeds.

COLORING

Medium coloring, usually blue, gray, or green eyes, from
sandy, blondish to medium brown hair.

DEPICTION

A woman of above coloring.

COMMENTS

Two and three queens indicates a "hen party," thus gossip,
a bridal shower, coffee and conversation, girl's club, a
women's liberation group, girl's school, Girl Scouts, etc.
Often read as the Mother card or a woman who is a
motherly type: affectionate, sympathetic, concerned for
the welfare of others. Seldom read as "the other woman"
in a layout . . . that is usually reserved symbolically (as
opposed to realistically) to the Queen of Pentacles and the
Queen of Swords.

Queen of Cups

King of Cups

DESCRIPTION

A king is seated on his throne holding a scepter in his left hand and a cup in his right hand. His throne seems to be "sitting on the sea." On his right side, a dolphin rises from the water while a ship is seen on his left.

SYMBOLISM

Water symbolizes the subconscious, thus a man who is in control of himself and kindly toward others.

COLORING

Medium coloring, usually blue, gray, or green eyes, from sandy to medium brown hair.

DEPICTION

A woman of above coloring.

COMMENTS

A fatherly man, father, big brother, friend of the family, minister, priest, more apt to be in the arts and sciences rather than in business or industry, a "family man," a "homebody," a "one-woman man." Can also signify a guru, swami, professor, occult teacher, sage, wise old man. Must be read in accordance with surrounding cards which will emphasize, modify, or refute the inherent meanings of this card.

King of Cups

WANDS

Element: Fire; Direction: South; Regular Deck: Clubs

Wands represent enterprise, work, labor, business and social contracts, tilling of the soil, harvest, effort, energy expended, "elbow grease," dedication and application to a job, "as ye sow so shall ye reap," business transactions, plans and projects, manufacturing, agriculture, industry, marketing, trades, labor unions, conferences, seminars, investments, securities, country clubs, parks, playgrounds, resorts, children's camps, communes, fraternities, sororities, political and religious organizations, co-operatives, "the great outdoors," classes (usually nonacademic, such as painting, writing, dancing, crafts, cooking, self-improvement, psychic development, occult arts, etc.).

The depicted wands are always shown with leaves. This represents life's constant renewal, budding ideas, enterprises, creativity. Whether the energy expended is worthwhile or the ideas sound depends upon surrounding cards. In medieval times wands represented the peasant (serf) class. He had to work for all he got. The king symbolizes the lowly born who is a "self-made man," one who has risen above his beginnings. Whether they're called wands, batons, rods, or clubs, they symbolize the "staff of life" (bread) acquired through effort.

Wands in a sense are an extension of self, i.e., the "tools of one's trade" whether the musician's baton, the magician's wand, the farmer's hoe, the carpenter's hammer, the churchman's scepter, the student's pencil, etc. It was through commerce and trade that the various peoples of the world got to know one another. It opened the doors of communication and cultural exchanges.

Ace of Wands

DESCRIPTION

The center of the card is dominated by a hand holding a flowering wand. A castle sits on a mountain peak in the distance.

MEANING

This card is the same as the Ace of Clubs. Numerically equivalent to number one. A beginning, start, origin. Wands refer to business and social matters. Specifically, the start of a new business matter or a social beginning, a telephone call, message, invitation, or telegram. A letter containing business news, data, an application, or financial statement.

RHYMED MESSAGE

> Ace of Wands is a message or call
> Important, so "get on the ball."

COMBINATIONS

Surrounded by Cups and Pentacles, Ace of Wands brings happy news. Surrounded by Swords, the news is bad. This card means communication in one form or another. Can mean lack of communication. Wands in and of themselves are neutral cards. Whether good or bad is determined by other cards (Cups and Pentacles are positive, while Swords are generally negative). Falling next to The Tower, it means an enterprise that "never gets off the ground." Same meaning near Death, "died aborning." Can mean a false start if the other cards are Cups or Pentacles. Near The Devil, indicates someone secretly envious, resentful, working against you.

Ace of Wands

Two of Wands

DESCRIPTION

A man is holding a wand in his left hand and a globe in his right. He seems to be looking at the sea. Another wand (or staff) is secured by a ring to a wall. The left side of the card has a drawing of roses and lilies.

MEANING

The man seems to be a property owner, a businessman. Indicates a business partnership, a business letter, small deal, minor transaction, a "man of the world" looking forward for other worlds to conquer. A time card meaning "within a two" whether two days, weeks, or months.

RHYMED MESSAGE

> Two of Wands means "There's no time like now"
> To get things done and learn the "know-how."

COMBINATIONS

When surrounded by Swords, may indicate "Time's running out." With the Ten of Wands, may indicate someone in manufacturing, especially dealing in clothes fabrics, or connected with the garment industry. Swords near this card indicate partnership troubles, discord, conflicting interests and attitudes. Falling near The Tower, indicates a feeling of disaster, usually caused by bad news (like a bank refusing to extend credit or grant a much-needed loan). Falling near The Emperor or The Empress, the chance to rise to the top, to be head of one's own business, president of a company.

Two of Wands

Three of Wands

DESCRIPTION

A man with his back turned is holding a wand in his right
hand while two other wands are standing upright. On the
horizon there's an outline of mountains, in front of which
are ships sailing the sea.

MEANING

This indicates commerce, trade, possibly in the import-
export business, overseas transactions, a partnership con-
sisting of three persons, a business that starts small but has
the seeds of growth, a small social club, plans for business
expansion.

RHYMED MESSAGE

> Three of Wands or the three-leaf clover
> Get down to business . . . look things over!

COMBINATIONS

If this falls next to The Tower, it spells disaster. If near the
Wheel of Fortune, the beginning of a profitable enterprise.
If near The High Priestess, the first step toward initiation
in the Higher Mysteries. If near The Fool, "Watch your
step." If near The Lovers, represents an unexpected love
affair, and if there are Sword cards preceding or after this,
a warning not to mix business with pleasure. If it falls near
The Moon, it means long hours, working late into the night.
If surrounded by Cups and Pentacles with Justice nearby,
it says that this self-sacrifice will pay off in the long run.

Three of Wands

Four of Wands

DESCRIPTION

Four budding wands are standing upright with a garland of flowers at their top. Two women are lifting flowers above their heads. They are near a bridge over a moat which leads to the castle shown in the background.

MEANING

Solidly laid plans, stability, a firm foundation. Symbol of architecture, building, engineering, planning, leaving "no stone unturned," and making sure that all sides are covered before embarking on any venture. The Four of Wands specifically can mean a car, conference table, desk, drawing board, and constructive work of any kind (woodworking, cabinetmaking, window dressing, etc.).

RHYMED MESSAGE

> Four of Wands is always constructive
> Learning to drive is also instructive!

COMBINATIONS

If near Death, it means specifically a coffin or a business failure. If near The World, the chance that one can have a worldwide business enterprise. If near The Magician, a new invention. When this card falls near The Hermit, it means that one does his best work alone (the artist, inventor, writer, etc.). If this falls near The Moon, it symbolizes a "night person" who does his best work after the sun goes down. If this falls near The Star, it means he will realize his ambitions, achieve his goals.

Four of Wands

Five of Wands

DESCRIPTION

Five young men seem to be having a stick fight but there is no sign of actual bodily combat.

MEANING

Aggressiveness, competitiveness, struggle, strife, differences of opinion, verbal fights (as opposed to physical). The need to "take things into one's own hands," to try to obtain cooperation from others but not be blocked if this is not forthcoming. The midway point in a business or social situation where certain things have to be brought out into the open and discussed, especially those things that are potentially unpleasant. A small amusement place, restaurant, bar, or cocktail lounge where social and business contacts are made.

RHYMED MESSAGE

> Five of Wands is the place that relaxes
> After paying your income taxes!

COMBINATIONS

If this falls near Death, The Tower, or high Sword cards it means warring factions, irreparable and irreconcilable disagreements (loss of a job or a business breakup). Surrounded by The Sun, The Star, or the Wheel of Fortune, it indicates competitiveness that will promote growth. The Hermit near this card says that it is better to "go it alone." The Devil would indicate that it is a waste of time to try to reconcile differences since opposing parties are not receptive to this.

Five of Wands

Six of Wands

DESCRIPTION

A man is shown riding a horse accompanied by others (footmen) who carry wands. He holds only one wand and wears a laurel wreath on his head (a symbol of victory). Another such wreath rests on his wand.

MEANING

Simply read, this represents victory, triumph, winning out, the successful completion of a task, venture, business deal, etc. Take another look at the Five of Wands, which precedes this card. He has passed the midway point, met and overcome the crisis, won out in the struggle for power, is given full backing and support. Most of the opposition is now united under one banner and ready to forge ahead and go about the business at hand.

RHYMED MESSAGE

> Six of Wands means getting the job done
> Now you can concentrate on having some fun.

COMBINATIONS

If this falls near The High Priestess, it means that there is more time for interest in spiritual, psychic, or occult matters (also true of The Magician to a lesser degree). If it falls near The Hierophant, indicates a businessman (or woman) who may be a heavy contributor to his church and possibly hold some kind of honorary office. If this card is surrounded by Sword cards, it says that there are still more problems ahead. The Fool near it is a warning to beware of "a fool's paradise" and not to let the temporary triumph go to his head—enemies are still at work. Near The Moon, it means to hold his position—he will have to "burn the midnight oil."

Six of Wands

Seven of Wands

DESCRIPTION

Grasping a budding wand with both hands, a young man stands on a hill. Six other similar wands stand upright in front of him.

MEANING

All sevens imply change. This card specifically indicates that one must hold his own against unfavorable odds, to take a stand, to be adamant and uncompromising in the face of opposition. In change there's growth and in all growth change is inevitable. Can be read as an office, business building, the stock exchange. It carries with it a subtle warning that one must "take a break" and not be preoccupied with business seven days a week, or it will take its toll. He needs that seventh day to relax, replenish his energies, and recharge his batteries!

RHYMED MESSAGE

> Seven of Wands is a change for the better,
> In business or a social matter.

COMBINATIONS

Whether the change in business is good or bad again depends upon surrounding cards. If this is near The Lovers followed by Sword cards, there's a warning that business or social matters may be disrupting his personal or home life (marriage, wife, children, etc.). If near The Hanged Man, indicates that he may need to change his ways or reverse his position. Temperance near it is telling him to "slow down, take it easy," while Death is warning him, "You're killing yourself."

Seven of Wands

Eight of Wands

DESCRIPTION

Eight budding wands dominate this card. Against a blue background (sky) they seem to be flying in the air and ready to descend to the country scene below.

MEANING

A small business trip, "shop talk," business discussion, the ability to affect harmony and balance in business by "weighing one's words," using tact and diplomacy, balancing the budget, "in the black" financially, keeping things on an even keel. Socially, the ability to pass smoothly from one group to the next. Generally a conversation card, indicating lots of talk, discussion, debate.

RHYMED MESSAGE

> Eight of Wands means "Talking up a storm!"
> Balancing the budget . . . true to form!"

COMBINATIONS

If this falls near Sword cards or near The Tower, The Devil, or Death it means that you have "put your foot into your mouth." You may have talked yourself into trouble. It means indiscretion, betrayal of confidence, loose talk that can be used against you. Near The Sun, it represents wit, brilliance, eloquence. Near The Moon, secret discussion, whisperings, gossip; and with other Sword cards, character assassination. Near The Lovers, it is "sweet talk," compliments, being told "I love you." Near The Devil, symbolizes being verbally seduced, temptation, double-talk.

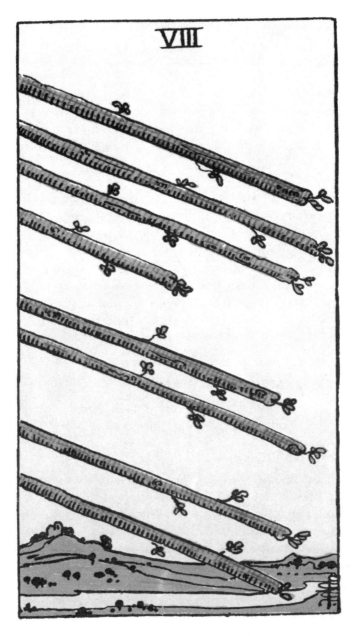

Eight of Wands

Nine of Wands

DESCRIPTION

A man stands alone with a bandage around his head. He is holding one budding wand while behind him are eight other upright wands. Mountains are in the background.

MEANING

It can be just as lonely at the top as on the bottom. One must protect, guard, and defend his resources, his property, his gains. Specifically, a profitable business opportunity, a lump sum of money, a big business deal. Getting to the top in one's business or job, an executive position, earning a top salary, the man able to delegate authority and to keep things in running order in a business, corporation, or institution; the need to "hold one's own" while being "up front" and see to it that things are run systematically.

RHYMED MESSAGE

> Nine of Wands refers to a Big Deal
> You're on your way Mister "Big Wheel."

COMBINATIONS

Nine of Wands with the Ten of Wands (sometimes the Four of Wands) indicates the building trades, real estate, buying and selling of property. With The Chariot, someone who works in, on, or with vehicles. With The Magician, may mean a business dealing in occult supplies, books, magic apparatus. Near The Lovers, a bridal shop, catering service, banquet hall, romance items, talismans, books, magazines. Near The Sun, travel bureaus, resort agencies, vacation spots, tourist hotels, playgrounds, outdoor recreation areas. Near The Moon, businesses that operate at night: hotels, nightclubs, bars, theaters, etc.

Nine of Wands

Ten of Wands

DESCRIPTION

A man is carrying ten wands and heading toward the city. He's bent down under the burden, literally "has his hands full."

MEANING

Overworked, burdened by responsibilities, a thriving business, "up to my ears in work," an implication of "all work and no play" but not necessarily bad if that's one's goal, on a social merry-go-round, attending one party or gathering after another (which may or may not combine business-professional contacts, reasons, goals). Short business trip.

RHYMED MESSAGE

Ten of Wands whether business or pleasure
The Wheel of Fortune spins you a treasure!

COMBINATIONS

Near The Star, sure to realize your goals. Near The Hanged man and Sword cards, indicates that you will practically have to stand on your head to get things done. If this falls near Strength it means that though tired and frustrated, you will be able to tap an inner reservoir of energy to acocmplish what you set out to do. This card near The Wheel of Fortune indicates progress, prosperity, success. Surrounded by Swords, means business turmoil, trouble, reverses. Surrounded by Cups and Pentacles, a "thriving business." If this card comes near The Fool, may indicate an error in judgement, a wrong decision, the result determined by what cards follow.

Ten of Wands

Page of Wands

DESCRIPTION

A young man (page) holds a budding wand in his hands. In the background there are mountains or possibly pyramids.

SYMBOLISM

A messenger (like our senate pages).

COLORING

Medium dark, brown eyes, light to dark brown hair.

DEPICTION

A young child, a teenager, an adolescent, may be either a boy or a girl.

COMMENTS

The sexual ambiguity of this card in most descriptions is not borne out by the illustration. Read it generally as a young boy or teenager. May imply someone who works as a messenger, runs errands, a dark young man in or around the family, the beginning of sexual awareness.

Page of Wands

Knight of Wands

DESCRIPTION

A knight dressed in armor is mounted on a horse that has its two front legs raised in the air. The knight carries a short budding wand in his right hand. The background depicts pyramidal mountains.

SYMBOLISM

On the threshold of life, the time when a young man may have to leave home, make decisions, go out into the world.

COLORING

Medium dark, brown eyes, light to dark brown hair.

DEPICTION

A young man of above coloring.

COMMENTS

May represent the romantic interest or husband of a young woman. Two knights together means a legal or court case. "The knight in shining armor" of romanticism, the young man who will come into the life of the young woman being read if she hasn't a boyfriend, and especially if she's wishing to meet someone new.

Knight of Wands

Queen of Wands

DESCRIPTION

A crowned queen sits on her throne wearing royal robes.
The crest of two lions is above her, while two others form
the throne's arms. She holds a budding wand in her right
hand and a sunflower in her left. A cat sits in front of her.

SYMBOLISM

A woman who is "well off," secure, comfortable, "Queen
of all she surveys."

COLORING

Medium dark, brown eyes, light to dark brown hair.

DEPICTION

A woman of above coloring.

COMMENTS

She may or may not be married. May represent the person
getting the reading. The cat in front of her indicates that
she can be "catty" as well as like pets. Usually she is interested in and fond of any picture card that falls near her
(King, Knight, or Page). If near another Queen card, the
surrounding cards will indicate whether this is a friend,
an acquaintance, or a rival.

Queen of Wands

King of Wands

DESCRIPTION

A crowned king in royal robes is seated on a throne. He
holds a budding wand in his right hand. His cloak has
mystical symbols on it. The back of his throne has a lion
and lizardlike creatures on it. A lizard lies to the left side
of his feet.

SYMBOLISM

A business or professional man, secure, affluent, self-
confident, authoritative, sure of himself.

COLORING

Medium-dark skin, brown eyes, light to dark brown hair.

DEPICTION

A man of above coloring.

COMMENTS

In a layout with either two or three other kings this means
public recognition, publicity, being honored, a testimonial
dinner. Two kings indicates a partnership: implies sharing,
getting along, making profitable contacts, settling a deal
over a handshake. Whether he's single, married, divorced,
or widowed must be intuitively determined by surrounding
cards.

KING of WANDS

King of Wands

BIBLIOGRAPHY

Benjamine, Elbert. *Sacred Tarot.* Los Angeles: Church of Light, 1945.

Case, Paul Foster. *The Tarot: Key to Wisdom of the Ages.* New York: Macoy Publishing Company, 1947.

Crowther, Patricia & Arnold. *Secrets of Ancient Witchcraft With the Witches Tarot.* Introduction by Dr. Leo Louis Martello. Secaucus: University Books, 1988.

de Lawrence, L. W. *The Illustrated Key to the Tarot,* Chicago, 1916.

Foli, P.R.S., *Card Fortune Telling at a Glance.* Baltimore: I. & M. Oppenheimer, 1953.

Levi. *Transcendental Magic.* 1896, repub. by Rider & Co., London, 1958.

Martello, Leo Louis. *It's in the Cards.* New York: Key Publishing Co., 1964.

Martello, Leo Louis, *It's in the Stars.* New York: Key Publishing Co., 1965.

Martello, Leo Louis. *Witchcraft: The Old Religion.* Secaucus: University Books, 1988.

Martello, Leo Louis. *How to Prevent Psychic Blackmail.* New York: Hero Press, 1966; repr. Samuel Weiser, 1975.

Martello, Leo Louis. *Weird Ways of Witchcraft.* New York: HC Publishers, 1969.

Martello, Leo Louis. *Hidden World of Hypnotism.* New York: HC Publishers, 1969.

Martello, Leo Louis. *Black Magic, Satanism & Voodoo.* New York: HC Publishers, 1972.

Martello, Leo Louis. *Curses in Verses.* New York: Hero Press, 1971.

Papus. *Tarot of the Bohemians.* London: Rider & Co., 1910.

Rakoczi, Basil Ivan. *The Painted Caravan.* The Hague: L.J.C. Boucher, 1954.

Schmaltz, John Barnes. *Nuggets From King Solomon's Mines.* Boston: Barta Press, 1908.

Spence, Lewis. *Encyclopedia of Occultism.* Secaucus: University Books, 1960.

Waite, Arthur Edward. *The Pictorial Key to the Tarot.* Secaucus: University Books, 1959.

ABOUT THE AUTHOR

Dr. Leo Louis Martello has a varied and extensive background as an author, graphologist, hypnotist, and civil rights activist. His grandmother and great-grandmother were Sicilian witches, and he was influenced by them. Dr. Martello became an ordained minister, then resigned to devote himself to research into philosophy, psychology, and the Old Religion (witchcraft). He is also the founder and director of the Witches Anti-Discrimination Lobby.

In 1970 Dr. Martello tried to obtain permission to hold a Witch-In in New York's Central Park but was refused. Backed by the American Civil Liberties Union, he threatened to file a suit, claiming discrimination against a minority religion. The Parks Department reversed its stand, a permit was granted, and the first civil rights victory for witches in history was won. A documentary film was made of the Witch-In by Global Village.

Dr. Martello has appeared on numerous radio and television programs, lectures extensively, and has been published in over 300 magazines. His work has been noted in over fifty books, including *The Encyclopedia of Witches and Witchcraft, Who's Who in the Psychic World*, and *Crossroads: Who's Who in the Magickal Community*. Dr. Martello is currently contributing editor of *The Rosegate Journal*, the official report medium for the Witches Anti-Defamation League.

In the past, Dr. Martello has been treasurer of the American Graphological Society, director of The American Hypnotism Academy, pastor of the Temple of Spiritual Guidance, director of Hero Press, and publisher of the *Wica Newsletter* and *Witchcraft Digest*. He has authored many books, including *Witchcraft: The Old Religion, How to Prevent Psychic Blackmail, Hidden World of Hypnotism, Black Magic, Satanism and Voodoo, It's in the Cards, It's in the Stars, Curses in Verses*, and *Weird Ways of Witchcraft*.

For those interested in knowing more about the Old Religion of Witchcraft, send a stamped, self-addressed envelope to Dr. Leo Louis Martello, Suite 1B, 153 West 80th Street, New York, NY 10024.

INDEX